Foreword

One of the central activities of an art museum is the acquisition of works for its permanent collection. The purpose of this activity is not merely to accumulate as many works as possible. A museum's decision to acquire an object is dictated, instead, by its curatorial and educational mission. For a museum like The Art Institute of Chicago, a permanent collection is a vast resource that serves both the general public and the scholarly community. Each new work in the museum reveals another aspect of the history of art; each acquisition elaborates the story that the collection tells.

Over the last century, the Art Institute has built a collection of great breadth and quality through a collaboration among donors, collectors, curators, administrators, and trustees. The museum continually displays a significant portion of this collection, thereby fostering a relationship between the museum's visitors and its extensive body of works. The permanence of this collection means that a visitor can return to particular works again and again. Each encounter with a work can reveal a new meaning or a previously unnoticed detail; in this way, the multiple meanings of a work can unfold gradually for a visitor in the museum's serene and hospitable setting.

This issue of *Museum Studies* is an opportunity to document and appreciate the fruits of the Art Institute's more recent collecting activities. All of the principal works examined in this issue have been acquired since 1980. They were selected by James N. Wood, Director and President of the Art Institute, who considered many masterworks acquired during his tenure at the museum before making this selection. Because of space considerations, this issue includes recent acquisitions in only half of the Art Institute's curatorial departments: Africa, Oceania, and the Americas; Asian Art; European Decorative Arts and Sculpture; Photography; and Twentieth-Century Painting and Sculpture. The other departments—American Arts, Architecture, European Painting, Prints and Drawings, and Textiles—will be represented in a future issue of *Museum Studies*.

The subjects of the essays in this issue, which range from African sculpture to American photography, attest to the diversity of the museum's acquisitions since 1980. Our first essay focuses on a drum created by a master Senufo sculptor of the Ivory Coast in West Africa. Anita J. Glaze of the University of Illinois at Urbana-Cham-

paign closely examines the iconography of this drum to reveal the sculptor's complex allusions to Senufo rituals, customs, and history. As Glaze explains, the standing female figure supporting the drum represents the great responsibility that Senufo women often bear, particularly during ceremonial events. Some of the bas-relief motifs on the Art Institute's drum—such as a snake seizing a fish or another snake attacking a tortoise—refer to the conflicts and competition that are part of the Senufo people's daily life. The carved images of manacles and warriors allude to the wars that have afflicted the Senufo people in the past. These correspondences, however, tell only part of the story, for each element has more than one meaning, and each element relates to others in the drum's design. As Glaze explicates the elaborate imagery of this drum, she leads us into the fascinating world that produced it.

One of the outstanding works to enter the Art Institute's collection in the last decade is Constantin Brancusi's *Golden Bird*. As Margherita Andreotti, Associate Editor at the Art Institute, explains in our second essay, *Golden Bird* is the crowning achievement of Brancusi's experiments with the avian form. *Golden Bird* was, in both its form and its subject matter, a radical break from the tradition of figural sculpture exemplified by Auguste Rodin. Brancusi's sculpture, however, won acclaim from contemporary intellectuals and eventually influenced generations of sculptors who followed. Andreotti places *Golden Bird* in the context of Brancusi's early career and his long series of *Birds*, and she delves into the intriguing origins of the base on which the sculpture now stands.

We turn next to an ornate upright piano designed by the British designer Mackay Hugh Baillie Scott. Ghenete Zelleke, Associate Curator of European Decorative Arts at the Art Institute, explores the career of Baillie Scott and the debate over interior design among British designers during the late nineteenth century. Baillie Scott was a member of the Arts and Crafts Movement, which called for artists to craft their works by hand and to shun modern techniques of mass production. The Art Institute's piano also embodies another Arts and Crafts precept—to be beautiful as well as practical. Zelleke shows that Baillie Scott succeeded brilliantly in overcoming the technical challenge of creating a handcrafted, aesthetically pleasing musical instrument.

Constantin Brancusi's *Golden Bird* (1919/20), one of the Art Institute's most important acquisitions of the last decade, occupies a prominent place in the museum's recently remodeled galleries of modern art. On the right is Henri Matisse's celebrated masterpiece *Bathers by a River* (1909–16), which the Art Institute acquired in 1953.

In our fourth essay, James T. Ulak, Associate Curator of Japanese Art at the Art Institute, examines five Japanese masterworks. The first of these is an enigmatic sixteenth-century portrait of Daruma, the semilegendary founder of Zen Buddhism, which depicts the Zen patriarch in rich, sensual colors. Ulak then turns to a seventeenth-century pair of screens entitled *Millet Under the Aspects of Sun and Moon*, which, in its blend of Buddhist, literary, and scientific influences, is a superb example of Japanese screen painting. The last works discussed in the essay are three dramatic woodblock prints by the master Katsushika Hokusai that portray fishing scenes; as Ulak explains, these works were part of a movement to create popular landscape prints after the Japanese government began to censor other kinds of images at the end of the eighteenth century.

The final essay discusses the work of Paul Strand, one of the most accomplished and celebrated photographers of our time. Using *Fall in Movement*, one of Strand's late still lifes, as his starting point, David Travis, Curator of Photography at the Art Institute, examines Strand's long career as a quest to develop an "objective" technique. As Strand photographed southwestern American landscapes, Mexican villagers, and details of machines, he tried to expunge obvious signs of his personality from each work.

Travis explores the paradox of creating art objectively even as one develops a recognizable—and, therefore, personal—style. *Fall in Movement* is a particularly salient example of this paradox, for its elegiac qualities reflect Strand's old age even as he attempted to represent only the natural qualities of the foliage before his camera.

The works selected for this issue are not only fine examples of their types, but benchmarks of the high standards that the Art Institute upholds in its quest to create the most comprehensive and satisfying collection possible. The superlative quality of these works demonstrates the museum's commitment to surprise, delight, and challenge its audience with each new acquisition.

MICHAEL SITTENFELD

Editor

Call and Response:
A Senufo Female Caryatid Drum

ANITA J. GLAZE

Associate Professor of Art History
University of Illinois at Urbana-Champaign

The Art Institute of Chicago has been fortunate to add to its African collection a female caryatid drum that is the work of a Senufo master sculptor of consummate technical skill and aesthetic sensibilities (pl. 6 and figs. 3–4). A single-membrane drum is supported by a seated female figure, a rare elaboration of a basic four-legged drum type that is used in a wide variety of contexts among the Senufo. The elongated resonating chamber is embellished with lively designs carved in bas-relief. The artist's conception combines formal strength with a philosophical complexity that springs from the relationship of the two principal iconographic components, the female figure and the panel of bas-relief images. Occasionally, one encounters a painting or sculpture that seems to epitomize the period or culture that produced it, and this is such a work.

The Senufo people of West Africa are the largest in the Gur language family, numbering about one and a half million people, including the northern branches in Mali and Burkina Faso and the central and southern branches in Côte d'Ivoire (or the Ivory Coast) (see fig. 2). Senufo traditional culture is based on subsistence agriculture supplemented by hunting, and it is historically linked with western Sudanic blacksmith technology.

Most Senufo art is commissioned by the membership of two gender-linked institutions that, along with matrilineal kinship structures, constitute the foundations of Senufo traditional culture. The Poro Society is an initiation society for young people of both genders and a village regulatory society under the control of male elders. Poro elders are responsible for important ancestral rituals as well as closely guarded secrets of defensive magic. The Sandogo Society is an organization of women representing specific matrilineage segments, a sacred institution that the Senufo believe was given by the creator god Kolocolo to facilitate communication between human society and the spiritual world. Sandogo members (*Sandobele*; singular, *Sando*) are said to be selected by the spirits, their nomination confirmed by divination. Each "matrilineal house" is represented by a woman Sando who is trained to serve as a spiritual mediator for their families; some are consecrated to this priestly role in early childhood. Not all Sandogo members become professional diviners who receive clients from outside family circles. In addition to the "matrilineal house" Sando, any number of women as well as men become Sandogo members as directed by controlling spirits through the process of supernatural encounters and divination.[1]

Senufo sculptors belong, by right of birth, to either the blacksmith artisan group or to the Kulebele, the much smaller and more specialized group composed strictly of woodcarvers. The name standardized in the literature as "Kulebele" has at least three regional variations, one of which is *Ku-lii-bele* (plural). The etymology of the word reveals something of artisan-farmer social history and attitudes. The root word *kulo* (world,

FIGURE I. A newly acquired *tyebinge* drum, carved by the popular sculptor Dunyime of Kobelio, is played by a young neophyte of the Tyekpa Society as a prelude to the arrival of the senior women initiates with their drums. The compositional structure of the drum, including the stool support and scalloped band that set off the panel, as well as the equestrian motif, are evidence of a general relationship with older traditions of bas-relief drum sculpture. Photo: Anita J. Glaze (Fodombele village, Korhogo district, March 1993).

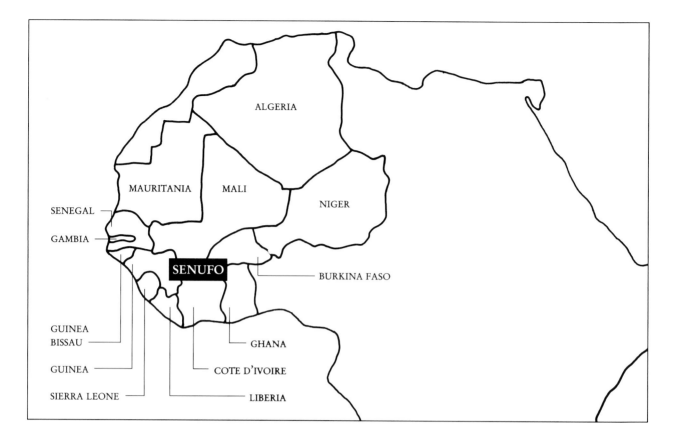

FIGURE 2. Northern Africa. Indicated here are the Senufo region of West Africa and the countries that surround it.

country, region) combined with the verb *lii* (to eat) means literally "those who eat off the regional people," a blunt comment on the landless status of the carvers. The name refers to both the sculptors' mobility and their dependence on the patronage of farmers for their livelihood.[2] Ambitious Kulebele sculptors habitually traveled wherever there were commissions and prosperous farmer-patrons to act as hosts. Moreover, young Kulebele would be sent to work as apprentices in other workshops, some in other regions. Yet all sculptors maintained close relationships with the oldest and larger Kulebele settlements where they had their own versions of the Poro secret societies.

The Kuleo master who carved the Art Institute's drum may have been working as early as the 1920s, although the drum was probably carved sometime during the 1930s or early 1940s. Kulebele migrations into northern Côte d'Ivoire began at least as early as the end of the eighteenth century. Oral history and genealogical records indicate that the Kulebele were established in San (twenty-five kilometers from the Mali border) around 1790, and perhaps earlier in Bolipe, the village that the eastern branch of Kulebele claim to be the oldest Kulebele settlement founded by immigrants from Mali. Oral history indicates that all major settlements of both western and eastern branches were established before

the Samoury Wars that began in the 1880s.[3] Local centers of style and family-based workshops developed among the western Kulebele in the Bagoe River valley along an axis that stretches from the Mali frontier to the Boundiali area about one hundred miles to the south. Abundant varieties of wood were available within these forest corridors. To the east, strong centers of style also flourished in the Kulebele settlements in the Mbengue region and, later, in Korhogo.

The iconography and style of the bas-relief motifs on the museum's drum are closely related to motifs carved in bas-relief on a number of doors, the best of which were carved primarily in the first third of this century by a small number of master sculptors from western Kulebele workshops, primarily those of Ouazumon, Dabakaha, and Kolia.[4] This area therefore appeared to be the most likely source of the drum pending confirmation in the field. Subsequent research among the Kulebele in both 1992 and 1993 indicated, however, that the western Kulebele of the Bagoe River valley had no memory of caryatid drums being carved in that region. By contrast, a few sculptors from eastern Kulebele settlements in the

Mbengue region were familiar with this rare variation of the more widely distributed four-legged standing drum, and were able to confirm the eastern provenance of caryatid drums.[5] Eastern Kulebele kinship and workshop networks include the ancient settlements at Bolipe, Kposurugo, and Kanonon in the Mbengue region, at Sienre and Sumo along its southwestern border, and at Korhogo to the south.

An eastern Kulebele attribution for the Art Institute drum has been substantially reinforced by a field photograph taken by a University of Illinois researcher that provides the only documentary evidence we have of a seated female caryatid drum still in a traditional village context (fig. 5). Significantly, the photograph was taken in 1981 in a village in the Kasara dialect area, whose residents, known as "Kasembele," are near neighbors of the Sienre, Sumo, and Mbengue Kulebele sculptors.[6] Identical in type and closely related in style, the Kasembele funerary drum belongs without question to the same workshop lineage as that of the two caryatid drums in the National Museum in Abidjan, Côte d'Ivoire, and the Art Institute. It is above all the more pictorial style of the bas-relief that proves the drum is from a later generation within a linear succession of master and followers. At the same time, its portrayal of a line of cultivators bending to their work, hoeing with a large *daba*, or men's hoe, suggests a historical unity with the four-legged drums associated with cultivating contests in the Nyene region to the northwest. Both the iconography and Dr. Thomas Bassett's contextual observations contribute toward a slowly emerging picture of distribution and usage patterns of the four-legged drum type, of which the caryatid would seem to be an innovative development that was originally confined to a relatively localized area among the Kasembele and Tagbanbele groups of Central Senufo farmers in the Mbengue region.

Of the four examples that appear in published collections, only the Art Institute drum and the one in the Abidjan collection are of significant age and usage.[7] A closely related caryatid drum, identified with the Nafara village of Sinematiali (thirty kilometers east of Korhogo), appears on a Côte d'Ivoire postal stamp issued in 1991 in the "Drums of Côte d'Ivoire" series. In 1970, because of increased Kulebele mobility and the economic success of the Kulebele production for export, the caryatid drum type surfaced as far south as a Kulebele workshop near Dikodougou, an area that has not yet been completely deforested by population pressure and is therefore attractive to Kulebele sculptors working for both traditional clients and the export market centered in Korhogo (see figs. 6–7).

The Senufo have for centuries bridged two broad stylistic regions—the western Sudanic to the north and the Guinea Coast to the south. Four-legged drums are a Guinea Coast musical and sculptural type that ranges from southern Guinea to equatorial Cameroon, including the Akan neighbors to the south of the Senufo in Côte d'Ivoire and in Ghana. Carved from a single block of wood, Senufo four-legged drums are elongated and vase-shaped above a stool-like support, and they are usually carved in bas-relief. As more than one Kuleo sculptor has explained, the bas-relief designs are intended to make a drum (or door) beautiful to behold and attractive to the client. From the sculptor's point of view, a principal reason for iconographic variation and selection is to demonstrate the ability and "intelligence" of the artist.

In its conception, the female figure on the Art Institute drum combines two traditional Senufo icons— seated female and load-bearing female—each of which has profound implications in Senufo culture. The female icon in itself resonates with meaning in Senufo culture, reflecting interlinking ideas of great complexity. Briefly, these include the concept of the biological priority of woman as founder of the family and a kinship system of matrilineal descent. Further, the titled female elder of any one matrilineage segment is usually the "mother" or head of the women diviners within the maternal family or *narigba'a* (or *nerege*). The role of women as spiritual mediators has its most important expression in the divinely ordained institution of the Sandogo Society, whose members are the guardians of orderly behavior and purity of lineage and are designated by the spirits to serve as vehicles of communication with God and lesser spirits. A belief in the spiritual powers of women is reflected in numerous masquerade and figural sculpture traditions that incorporate the female icon as an active guardian or protective force in contexts of intense competition or danger.[8] In the esoteric language of the Poro secret society, "Ancient Woman" or "Ancient Mother" (*Kacelëëò* or *Malëëò*) is both sacred spirit and spiritual sanction for male leadership and authority in the Poro organization as it follows the "road of the ancestors." The terminology parallels the relative positions of "oldest woman" of a matrilineage segment and male family heads, who are maternal uncles or brothers and are referred to as *syèènlëèò* ("the old one," also meaning "ancestor" in some contexts).[9] The sacred grove precincts of the Poro Society are equivalent to the "courtyard" of *Kacelëëò*, the initiates are her "children," and her law a powerful force for the ordering of society and for justice.

Finally, the female form has aesthetic priority in that it is judged more beautiful than the male and therefore more effective as art. The seated female figure in particular has enormous popularity in Senufo art traditions and occurs in a wide diversity of contexts in which particular spirits, individuals, or groups are honored and praised. The combination of female beauty and a posture associated with honor and status presents an image considered eminently appropriate for use in the sculpture of praise. For example, seated female figures, polished to a luminous black sheen, are placed within dance circles at Poro ceremonies celebrating advancement in the age-grade cycle, or are carried by initiates singing to raise funds, or appear as dance sculpture supported on the heads of Tyekpa Society members during funerary rituals honoring one of their sisterhood.

To the Senufo, the load-bearing posture is a visual affirmation of character and social responsibility. This icon of the supporting female evokes any number of a Senufo woman's daily activities—bearing on her head a large ceramic water jar, or carrying heavy piles of firewood, baskets filled with grain, or an enormous netted bundle of ceramic pots made for sale at a distant marketplace. The image of woman as load-bearer has figurative meaning as well, for the load is a metaphor for the weight of responsibilities and the many hardships to be borne in the course of a woman's life, not least of which is childbearing. In short, the gesture praises strength and industry as dimensions of female beauty, and affirms the woman's contribution to productivity in human society.

The imagery of the female caryatid drum brings immediately to mind the ritual practice in many Senufo groups of Poro drums played by male drummers and carried by female bearers. The scene illustrated in figure 8 captures a moment in one of the most important of Senufo ceremonial events—the commemorative celebration called *kuumo* or "great funeral." *Kuumo* honors the ancestral dead and the elders of the community who have died over the previous few years. Hundreds of visitors gather to join in a festival that orchestrates many different dances, masquerades, and instrumental performance groups. In a fast-moving procession that winds around the different residential quarters of the village, a Poro Society initiate plays vigorous rhythms on a drum held aloft by a young, unmarried girl. She bears its considerable weight with the same poise and formalized gesture as the figure of the caryatid drum. Selected as drum-bearer for her ritual partner, the girl achieves individual recognition as she contributes to a communal event of great spiritual, social, and aesthetic significance. Gender pairing as an expression of cosmic and social order is pervasive in Senufo art and ritual, exemplified here by the pairing of male drummer and female carrier.

This ritual action provides a structure of support that is commemorated in the sculpture. The arms frame the head, which balances with ease the imposing weight of the drum. The framed face suggests inward-directed energy, a concentration on inner resources. The seated pose elevates her to a position of honor and praise. By combining this pose with that of the load-bearing woman, with its connotations of moral and social responsibility, the sculptor has created a work of great conceptual as well as visual power.

The original purpose of the Art Institute drum is unknown, but it would almost certainly have included a funerary context and was possibly an "inheritance" passed down within a family of economic or social importance. The four-legged drum embellished with bas-relief carving is used in a wide variety of contexts among the Senufo. In the northern Bagoe River valley, drums carved with motifs similar to those on the museum's drum were used in the context of fiercely competitive hoeing contests, and were used for songs of praise for the champion cultivators. In the Kafiri and Tangara dialect areas near Korhogo, the drum is associated with a dance (*co'omi*) of youths and young girls of premarital age celebrating advancement in the Poro Society initiation cycle. The "insult" songs and ritual contexts involve the competitive and sometimes confrontational relationship of junior and senior initiate classes. Among the Tangara and in the Mbengue region, the drum is associated with funerals of descendants of ruling or founding families, and is used to announce a death to all villagers

FIGURE 3. Côte d'Ivoire, Senufo culture. *Female Caryatid Drum* (side view of pl. 6), late nineteenth/early twentieth century. Wood and hide; h. 123 cm, diam. at top 63.5 cm. The Art Institute of Chicago, Robert J. Hall, Herbert R. Molner Discretionary, Curator's Discretionary, and Departmental funds; Arnold Crane, Mrs. Leonard Florsheim, O. Renard Goltra, Ada Turnbull Hertle, Marion and Samuel Klasstorner, Holly and David Ross, Departmental Acquisitions endowments; through prior gifts of various donors (1990.137). The Art Institute female caryatid drum is an extremely rare type of the sacred four-legged drums that are used in ritual and dance contexts among many different Senufo ethnic groups. In many ways, this extraordinary sculpture stands as a paradigm of Senufo thought and culture. A drum is itself an important theme in Senufo oral literature, in which drums and drum music function as metaphors of spirit-derived human creativity and civilization. This drum is notable for its rich iconography alluding to competing forces in both the spiritual and temporal realms.

FIGURE 4. Côte d'Ivoire, Senufo culture. *Female Caryatid Drum* (back view of pl. 6). Both the side view (fig. 3) and this back view of the Art Institute drum clearly illustrate the traditional stylization of the head—including the scooped-out, heart-shaped face and the forward thrust of the elongated jaw—that present-day sculptors associate with "the way our ancestors carved" in ancient Kulebele workshops. The head, breasts, and hips of the figure extend nearly to the outer diameter of the original cylinder cut from a tree or branch, and the dynamic relationship of curved and angular forms creates a uniquely Senufo rhythm of figurative style. The richly oiled patina of the drum indicates many years of use and displays the warm, reddish tones that underlie the black stain or are allowed to remain unblackened as a decorative detail.

FIGURE 5. A female caryatid drum, identical in type and closely related in style to the Art Institute drum, was documented in 1981 in a traditional context in a Kasembele village bordering the Mbengue region. In this village, the drum was associated with funerary announcements and ritual. The bas-relief designs are carved in a more pictorial style than those on the Art Institute drum, and feature as a central motif a line of bending cultivators working with the *daba*—short-handled hoes with large iron blades that are still used in Senufoland, where the champion cultivator is a culture hero. Photo courtesy of Dr. Thomas Bassett, University of Illinois (northern Côte d'Ivoire, 1981).

within the surrounding fields. Such drums, usually in the custodianship of the village chief, were linked to former "kings" or powerful local warlords in both the Nyene and Mbengue regions. Among the Fodombele in the Dikodougou district and around Korhogo, the drum is used by women in both the Tyekpa Society ("women's Poro") and the women's Sandogo Society in the context of commemorative funerals. Sandogo four-legged drums are bare of bas-relief ornamentation, which is appropriate to the austere sanctions governing those members set apart for the priestly role of divination.

The theme of gender confrontation and conflict dominates the songs composed by Tyekpa Society musi-cians. In figure 9, Tyekpa Society women dance in a circle around the four-legged drums played by drummers of virtuoso skill. Women drummers are extremely rare in black Africa, where membrane drums are usually associated with males. The alternating song leaders and other women of the dance circle sing in the "call and response" style widespread in Africa in which the group repeats the phrases selected by the lead singer. Most Tyekpa songs, which are in a secret language that only initiated women can understand, insult men's sexual parts and behavior. Secrecy and ritual license allow women to express freely their anger or frustration at circumstances outside their control.[10]

A comparison of numerous published examples of bas-relief drums reveals a certain consistency to iconographic motifs and image groupings that is not accidental and cannot be explained satisfactorily by the vague references to "primordial animals" or "mythological subjects" or "war scenes" that are typical of most published references to Senufo drums and doors.[11] The Art Institute drum presents a model example of the iconographic themes of beauty, praise, conflict, and competition that dominate Senufo drum relief carving. Saturated with multiple references and allusions, its rich iconography invites the viewer into a universe of meaning if he or she is steeped in Senufo visual and symbolic languages. Even for Senufo viewers, the degree of comprehension is largely dependent on their access to areas of knowledge governed by such factors as cult membership, initiation status and rank, age or gender restrictions, specialized training as a diviner or healer, and membership in a particular family or ethnic group.

In a drawing of the images that encircle the drum (fig. 10), the entire iconographic program becomes visible and the artist's conception is revealed. Motifs recalling scenes of war, slave raids, and colonial forced labor are juxtaposed with an array of zoological creatures that are all associated with water and with nature spirits. The sculptor has in essence provided the viewer with a choice of two main groups of visual motifs that express the same basic ideological theme—the importance of knowledge and power in a world of competing forces, both spiritual and temporal.

The war motifs portray an equestrian warrior with upright lance prepared for battle, a victorious warrior with upraised arm holding manacles for a captured slave or prisoner of war, and a small antelope horn of the type that is used as a container for protective medicine and sorcery, a supernatural weapon of war considered essential to success. Senufo oral histories still vividly recall the difficult years of forced labor under the superior power of colonial rule. Accounts are equally articulate about the suffering endured during some of the regional excesses of local warlords, as well as the murderous practices of African slave raiders and *jihads* ("holy wars") that in earlier times ravaged parts of Senufo country.

At issue is a principle of interpretation of Senufo iconography in general and bas-relief motifs on drums and doors in particular. To restrict a motif to one meaning is to ignore the Senufo love of words and motifs that are interchangeable symbols in the contexts of their oral literature and the visual arts. At one level, the stylized warriors and manacles are references to the historical past and recall to Senufo viewers the suffering of their ancestors during the nineteenth-century Sudanic wars and colonialism. But the sculptor's principal subject here was not history as such but rather the central theme of competing forces at play. Confrontation and the testing of relative powers, conflict and combat, enslavement and bondage, victory and defeat—all can be figuratively applied to competitive events and circumstances that are of far greater moment and importance to the Senufo than past history. Ritualized hoeing contests, age-grade competition in the men's society, and "battles" on the supernatural plane are all cases in point.

FIGURE 6. Soro Beh, a Kulco sculptor (eastern branch, Korhogo) apprenticed to his older brother, guest resident sculptor in a Fodombele village in the Dikodougou district. As one of the initial stages of carving a female caryatid drum, Beh is blocking out the principal masses of the sculpture with the largest size adze in a scaled set of three. Later, the artist will switch to the smaller blade widths for detail and finishing contours. Senufo sculptors have an intimate knowledge of the numerous tree species and woods suitable for any one project. Harder woods such as Senegal mahogany (*Khaya senegalensis*) are selected for major figure sculptures for the Poro Society because of their resistance to insects, although softer, lighter woods such as the Guinea cottonwood or the Bombax (*Celiba pertandra, Bombax brivicuspe*) are often preferred for large drums that must be carried and for the easier carving of bas-relief. Photo: Anita J. Glaze (1970).

The second group of motifs presents a number of zoomorphic subjects, which in the drawing read left to right as follows: a long-billed bird such as a crane or heron, a crocodile (often replaced by or interpreted as the monitor lizard), a snake that has seized a fish as its prey, a tortoise attacked by a small snake, a generic bird placed at an angle in the space below, and a large tortoise with outstretched neck. All of these animals are associated with the water spirits and all are in a devouring or contending posture, an iconographic configuration that serves as a metaphor for the nature of reality according to the Senufo worldview. From village to cosmos, the world is perceived as a potentially threatening arena where the relative strengths of visible and invisible forces, in both the natural and the supernatural spheres, are constantly in play.

The two remaining motifs—the smaller of the two birds and the squares etched with cross-hatched designs —seem peripheral to the central theme and were perhaps inserted for purely aesthetic reasons. The design is enhanced with the syncopated rhythm of the squares that interrupt the succession of figures and provide angular contrast to the more rounded zoomorphic and human forms. The small tilted bird was possibly added as a compositional device to fill an awkward space. One sculptor who was interviewed, Zonzerege, identified the squares with cross-hatching as "scarification patterns" added for decoration. It should be noted that they are also suggestive of the square leather amulet packets, which are engraved or dyed with geometric patterns, that are worn as protective amulets by the Senufo and other West African peoples.

The first Western observer to take note of Senufo four-legged drums was Father P. Knops, whose ethnographic notes compiled during his mission service in the Korhogo region from 1923 to 1935 remain the single most important documentation of Senufo culture during the period of initial European contact. In an invaluable cataloguing of drum bas-relief motifs observed nearly three-quarters of a century ago, Knops listed a range of subjects that has continued to dominate bas-relief drum

FIGURE 7. Soro Beh's drum (see fig. 6). After the carving is completed, it is ready for the application of a bright red dye made from the moist inner layer of a tree root (*caami*) that acts as a fixative, which stains black those areas of the surface painted with an iron-rich mud paste (taken from dried-out ponds). Those areas of the sculpture that are not covered with mud will retain the red tones. After the artist has washed and lavishly oiled with shea butter oil, the client arranges for the attachment of the animal hide membrane and the application of ritual paint and other materials if appropriate. Beh's design includes a crocodile or lizard seizing a fish, comparable to the snake and fish motif on the Art Institute drum. Photo: Anita J. Glaze (1970).

iconography until very recently. Knops identified only one context or purpose for this drum type, that of "war drum." In an article on African musical instruments, Knops described "war drums" as follows:

[The war drums are] furnished sometimes with human skulls and jawbones. Their dimensions can exceed one and one-half meters long and 40 to 60 c. in diameter. The largest are carried on the head by two men followed by the drummer. Reproduced on the cylindrical drums are mythical motifs, python, monitor lizard, tortoise, chameleon, fish, or war scenes, captives in chains, and equestrian mounted warriors [carved in bas-relief]. Constructed on a pedestal the war drum is placed in the village as protection against thieves and poisoners, but *without musical utilization* [italics added]: according to Senufo dialects, it is then called *pliwo* or *pliguewo*: its height can reach 1.25 m.: some are masterpieces of sculpture.[12]

Knops was clearly confusing two different object types—drum and pedestal. The confusion of typology and nomenclature introduced here has persisted in the literature and requires clarification. In a recent publication on the art of Côte d'Ivoire, one author incorrectly gives *pliwo'o* as the generic name for Senufo four-legged drums.[13] In actuality, *piliwo* refers uniquely to a major "fetish" of historical interest in the Korhogo area, an instrument of power represented by a complex construction of mixed materials that rested on a footed pedestal. This massive four-legged support was carved with bas-relief figures that are linked stylistically and conceptually to those found on bas-relief four-legged drums. A careful reading of Father G. Clamens's meticulous description of this fetish, published in 1953, confirms that it was an instrument of protection and detection of reputedly great powers. According to Clamens, the term *piliwo* applied above all to the pedestal. The

literal translation of its name, "Black (or dark) night," refers to its role of fearsome watchguard over the village throughout the night.[14]

Data collected in a wide variety of Senufo dialect areas clearly indicates that the generic Senufo word for any true membrane drum is *pinge*, a root word in most local Senufo names for their particular category of the four-legged drum type. For example, the Tyekpa drum is *tye-pinge*, just as the age-grade and cultivator association drums are *tonbinge*.

In *Die Kunst der Senufo* (1988), Till Förster translated *tonbinge* as "father drum," a linguistic error that is repeated by T. Garrard in *Art of Côte d'Ivoire* (1993).[15] "Father" drum, however, is patently inappropriate in the context of a Poro Society tradition that in some areas calls its most sacred funerary drum by the secret term "Old Woman," and calls ancestors by the secret name "Maternal Uncle," thus paralleling in the ritual nomenclature the matrilineal kinship structure of society. Senufo languages are tonal and therefore loaded with pitfalls for the unwary and the untrained Western ear. The same consonant-vowel sequence changes dramatically in meaning according to whether the vowel is high, mid, low, or a glide in tone. Moreover, vowel length (short or long) and vowel nasalization are two additional factors that determine meaning. In this case, the *ton* (high tone, nasal, short vowel) means "association," in contrast to *too* (high tone, long vowel) which means "father" or equally "paternal uncle."[16] I should note that the correct etymology of *tonbinge* ("association-drum") was confirmed in March 1993 by respondents in four different dialect areas, from the Kadile at Tingrela to the Tangara near Korhogo.

In a memorial edition of Knops's complete notes, certain important changes and additions to his discussion of "war drum" appear that are useful to an interpretation of drum motifs and contexts. "War drum" is described in much the same way as in the first version, but now the generic term for "war drum" is given as *gbin'pinge*. Additional war scene motifs are also noted: "armed foot-soldiers, [objects representing] spoils of war, iron manacles for prisoners, and funerary masks symbolizing slain warriors." Two war drum motifs—armed warriors and iron manacles—are represented on the Art Institute's female caryatid drum. Knops also provided a fascinating glimpse of the ritual preparation of both war drum and drummer in former times. He recorded that "newly made drums such as these were painted with the sacrificial blood of rams," and that a new drum was placed for a number of days in ritual isolation, enclosed in a hut along with its designated drummer who "was nourished with magical substances."[17] In this connection, it should be noted that the female caryatid drum in the National Museum in Abidjan bears extensive traces of sacrificial materials. In Senufo culture, any material item can take on the nature of a cult object, receiving periodic offerings and sacrifices to renew a supernatural power accumulated over time.

In the same description of "war drums," Knops asserted that after 1898 the war drum changed name and function following the French colonial intervention that put an end to intertribal conflicts. According to Knops, the *gbin'pinge* now fulfilled a different village function under the name *pliwo* and, henceforth, in a village courtyard "fulfilled the role of a nocturnal protector against thieves, adulterers, malevolent sorcerers" that, he was told, "would immediately strike them down."[18]

Apart from the confusion of two different kinds of objects discussed above, a historical hypothesis is raised here that merits reconsideration. Both the range and diversity of four-legged drum usage in Senufoland provide ample reason to question a linear development from "war drum" to all Senufo dance drums or funerary drums of the four-legged type, with or without bas-relief. This assumption implies that the original context of the first Senufo four-legged drums was that of war, and that all other purposes and contexts developed later during more peaceful times. This assumption by Knops, as yet unsupported by adequate documentary evidence, was resurrected in a recent catalogue entry on four-legged drums.[19] Contextual and iconographic data on bas-relief drums collected over a period of years within a number of different Senufo ethnicities and districts suggest that Knops's documentation of "war drum" iconography and context must be placed in a broader interpretive framework of combat, bondage, competition, and conflict. Confrontation and the testing of relative forces in arenas other than war is a leitmotif in Senufo culture.

Deep-seated religious beliefs and philosophy address conflict and competition on a number of planes—cosmic, spiritual, ethical, and social. Numerous categories of both human and zoomorphic motifs derive from this ideological matrix.

Two drum contexts of particular interest in this regard include cultivator contests and a dance linked to the Poro Society initiation cycle in some Senufo areas. *Tonbinge* is the correct name for the four-legged drums associated with both the cultivating associations in the Tingrela and Nyene regions as well as an important coming-of-age ritual in the Kafiri and Tangara dialect areas. Among the latter two groups, the drum is a central focus in a dance in the Poro ceremonial cycle called *co'omi* (fig. 1). Boys in the junior-grade class of Poro (*plaobele* or *co'obolo*, according to dialect) dance and sing with young girls of premarital status during nighttime celebrations in preparation for the approaching advancement ceremonies in the initiation cycle. While the boys delight in wearing all manner of fancy dress selected for color and flash, the girls wear long white loincloths with intricately woven borders. As in Sandogo symbolism, the color white signifies ritual and personal purity. The girl's beauty is enhanced by a traditional facial design, often represented in figural sculpture, created by inserting charcoal subcutaneously in delicate cuts beneath the eyes. The leader of the girls' class has the honor of being drum-bearer and is selected by the village chief. The music features songs that insult the senior initiates, which are sung in a time of ritual license for the younger initiates who for several years have been subject to the senior's rigorous instruction and discipline. In the Tangara area, the drum and dance is also associated with ritualized wrestling matches between the two male age grades who are competing for possession of a certain (secret) object.[20] Significantly, age-grade competition emerges as an important cultural theme in the setting for the drum in its appearance in both junior grade dances and cultivating contests.

The iconographic motif of manacles (*kpè'élégé*, low tone) is a stylized representation of the forged iron collars and shackles used for slave traffic and for captives taken in war. Needless to say, its connotations address a

FIGURE 9. Two women drummers playing melodic rhythms on two *tyebinge* funerary drums that are placed in the center of a dance circle formed by members of the Fodombele women's Tyekpa Society. Each of the supporting legs of the drum has a typical bent-knee stance and foot suggestive of figure sculpture and dance position. Bas-relief designs feature two Nile Monitor lizards and a tortoise (not seen in this view), which belong to the group of five aquatic animals said to belong to the nature spirits. Photo: Anita J. Glaze (Fodombele village, Dikodougou district, 1979).

FIGURE 10. Reading from right to left, the iconographic motifs carved in bas-relief on the resonating chamber of the drum are: decorative squares associated with ornamental body art and scarification patterns; a long-beaked bird such as a heron or ibis; an equestrian warrior holding a spear; a crocodile "biting" a section of the decorative border; a snake seizing or devouring a fish; a victorious warrior holding the manacles formerly used to fetter prisoners of war taken as slaves; a second bird; a small snake attacking a water turtle; an antelope horn used as a container for magical substances; and a tortoise with outstretched neck. Drawing by Karen Aldenderfer.

particular category of bondage or domineering force. In relation to drums associated with hoeing contests, the interpretation of this motif revealed an unexpected dimension of Senufo visual syntax: when applied to cultivating competitions, the intrinsically negative manacle sign becomes part of an iconographic pattern that includes positive themes of praise and accomplishment.

The concept of the "champion cultivator" as a culture hero is a central expression of the Senufo ethos that idealizes the moral and social responsibility of work. In the fields and in village celebrations, the verbal, visual, and musical arts affirm the spiritual and ethical foundations of work. Ego and individual achievement are rewarded within carefully defined boundaries of competition that encourage productivity and meet community economic needs. The champion-cultivator concept reflects the belief that aggressive male competition and ambition is ideally appropriate only within group structures and responsibilities. In the setting of grueling agricultural labor, praise songs, poetry, and music transform work into ritual. Drum songs play out the praise names of "lion" and "strong heart" to honor the moral values of endurance and perseverance objectified in the champions whose heroic traits encourage the younger and weaker to stretch their efforts, thereby ensuring that fields will be planted in time for the seasonal rains.

In the Kadile dialect area around Tingrela and the large "Nyene" region of the Tyebala Senufo, the music and imagery of bas-relief drums provided an aesthetic and motivational setting for the cultivator competitions. Such images as a warrior decapitating his enemy or taking prisoners are popular iconographic themes on the

"association drum" (tonbinge). Symbols of mortal conflict and heroic victories are especially appreciated in the figurative sense. Icons of "master/slave" or "warrior/ captured prisoner" relationships are readily applied to the triumphant victory of "champions." In reference to the manacles motif, one Kadile respondent explained: "If I am champion, you see, I look at this design and I want to rule the others—I want them to be my slaves in the work."[21] The equestrian warrior evoked memories of "life and death battles" between regional champions of wide repute and the use of "medicine totems" or cultivator magic for self-protection and attack. "Killing" —that is, dominating—one's opponent in a fierce hoeing contest was contrasted with the humiliating defeat of competitors and the "destruction" of family honor and name. Among the Kadile, the return of the cultivators to the village after the day's competition is announced from afar by the calling tones of the drum. Parents and lovers hurry to the central dance area to learn if it is their child or special friend who has been named "the lazy one," "the last of his or her class." The disgrace of earning the pejorative title for even one day is enough to motivate the "lazy ones" to improve their ways. In contrast to most central Senufo people, in this northern region (Tingrela and the "Nyene" region) young people of both genders form cultivating associations.

Champion cultivator lore throughout the central Senufo groups is eloquent on the critical role played by "cultivator medicine" passed on from elders to favorite contenders in hoeing contests. The placement on the Art Institute drum of the antelope horn motif, a direct reference to individual instruments of power (*yasungo*), next to the image of the contending water snake and tortoise reflects the relationship of success in important hoeing contests and the knowledge of "medicine" and sorcery. Traditionally, cultivator drums as well as "king's drums" (heirlooms of ruling families) and war drums all received periodic sacrifices to replenish their powers and as a part of ancestral and spirit worship. The female caryatid drum in the National Museum collection in Abidjan bears evidence of frequent sacrificial anointings.

As noted earlier, only one example of a female caryatid drum identical in type to the Art Institute's drum has thus far been observed in context. The fact that the principal subject of its bas-relief carving explicitly depicts hoeing cultivators has special significance in reconstructing an iconology of the images carved on the Art Institute's drum. The more esoteric nature of this older drum's iconography is characteristic of traditional Senufo art and obscures for the outsider the subtle cross-references to cultivating "wars" and magic. The two motifs of serpents seizing a weaker prey—the one devouring a fish (or frequently a frog or toad) and the other contending with a round tortoise of equal size —have multiple applications in Senufo symbolism. One of these is demonstrably that of contending champion cultivators, particularly when viewed in the context of a bas-relief drum and in conjunction with war motifs. In the Kadile and Tyebala areas where bas-relief drums figure largely in cultivation contexts, the meaning was said by some Senufo respondents to be obvious and simple. Both the motif of a snake seizing a frog and that of the tortoise attempting to escape the snake were explained as referring to inherently antagonistic and competing strengths: "When you see the serpent and the toad, that means that certain people are never in agreement; if I am a cultivator that means that I hope to bite the others, devour the others."[22]

A second connotation of the manacles sign, familiar to any Senufo adult with much experience in consulting Sando or other diviners, concerns conflict and bondage in the context of spiritual warfare. Briefly, the manacles design is one of a core set of miniature divination signs forged in iron, which diviners commission from local blacksmiths (see fig. 11). Passed down through several generations of Sando diviners in the *nèrigè*, or maternal family, the sets are generally only one category of a group of fifty or more coded signs that each Sando uses in the process of divination. If the manacles sign falls next to one or two other designated signs, one of which represents the client, then further "throws" of a portion of the signs are made in order to verify this communication from the diviner's intermediary spirits who "speak" through the coded patterns of sign distribution. The client is either in danger or may already have been "captured" or placed under the control of a particular malevolent spirit, sorcerer, or someone of "two hearts" who wishes misfortune for the victim. Differently marked cowrie shells identify the specific source of danger. Further throws of the signs will direct the client as to which ritual actions should be taken for protection or healing.[23] For example, a tiny brass casting of the manacles icon may be attached as a *yawiige*, or protective charm, to an infant's ankle or waist.

War, battles of strength and skill, spiritual conflict— these three separate associations of the manacles motif, one literal and the other two figurative, serve to illustrate an important principle of iconographic analysis in respect to Senufo art. Since the same motif may have several analogous connotations, a correct interpretation of a particular visual sign, such as manacles, a female figure, or a serpent, requires a knowledge and understanding of typological and contextual settings.

The theme of competing powers, as represented by contending or devouring reptiles, birds, and occasionally an antelope, monkey, or other creature, has its most frequent application in the context of sorcery and divination. It reflects a philosophy that views the world as a dangerous arena in which supernatural resources are essential for securing health, wealth, and prosperity. Individuals, particularly those in positions of leadership, are responsible for securing the means of defending their own or their group's interests in the face of hostile agents or spirits that work in visible and invisible ways. Divination, especially the sacred institution of Sando diviners, represents the most important means of ascertaining the hidden causes of events or threatening circumstances.

The Senufo believe that, beyond the external, material appearances of nature, there are spiritual beings and other supernatural forces and energies at work that affect human welfare and destiny. These include the creator deity, who has priority and supreme authority, as well as guardian spirits (*yirigefòlò*), ancestral spirits, twin spirits, and the *ndebele* (*tugule* or *madebele* in some dialects) or nature spirits. One of the steps that a young boy takes as he approaches maturity is when he first visits a diviner or begins to receive instruction from an elder relative in the science of creating personal "fetishes" (*yasungo*), which are secretly constituted instruments of power and protection.

The core set of zoomorphic images that relate to the domain of spirits, divination, and sorcery is composed entirely of reptiles that are all associated directly or indirectly with water. As one venerable elder explained, "Monitor lizard, crocodile, tortoise, softshell turtle and python are the animals of the nature spirits (*ndebele*)— they are of the same *nèrigè* or matrilineal family."[24] As a former Sando diviner, this man's special totem was a monitor lizard, the form in which a spirit of the *nikan'ao* type had first appeared to him. The root word of this category of controlling spirit comes from a word that means "to astonish" and to "transform into something else." Once such a spirit "attaches" itself to a person, it is for life. Such spirits can provide powers and gifts, but typically they make difficult demands that increase in scale over time. *Ndebele* include water spirits and those classed as *nikan'abele* and the terms are often used interchangeably.

The Nile crocodile (*wocóòn*, high/low tone), or more commonly the Nile monitor lizard (*paaòn*, low tone), is considered to be the strongest and most powerful of the water animal family. This is apart from the python, which is a primary symbol in Senufo religion, and whose importance as spiritual mediator between heaven and earth transcends the rest of the water animal family and indeed the *ndebele* spirits themselves. The python motif is the primary insignia of Sandogo members. The crocodile is a favored symbol of personal or corporate male power as reinforced by association with or control of various supernatural resources. It is encountered in a wide range of forms, including bas-relief designs on earthen archi-

tecture (for example, Poro initiation houses, or personal shrines), on cast-brass ornament, on earthen sculpture in Poro sacred groves, and as openwork designs cut into flat wooden ceremonial headdresses worn by Poro Society initiates in some areas. *Paaòn* is also a favorite motif painted on the interior of shrines housing the materials of magic and divination, but it is largely seen only in the more elaborate constructions owned by male diviners of varying categories, including men called into divination by a spirit of the *nikan'ao* type. The Nile monitor lizard (*Varanus nilotieus*) can reach over a meter in length and is known to favor crocodile eggs as food. One aspect of its life cycle and breeding behavior may be significant in terms of its association with water, fertility, and nature spirits: the female lays her eggs inside the hard protective shell of termite nests, which only the heavy rains at the beginning of the rainy season soften enough to allow the scores of hatchlings to emerge.[25] The beginning of the rainy season is the peak time for worship and sacrificial offerings, a critical period in the ritual and agricultural calendar when heads of families and owners of fields solicit the favor of the spirits for success in planting and harvest.

Closely related to the crocodile motif in the composition of images carved in bas-relief on the Art Institute's drum is the turtle or tortoise, another important water animal and spirit messenger (see fig. 10). The behavior and habitat of the local species suggest several reasons why the tortoise is such an important symbol in Senufo iconography and mythology.[26] Tortoises may be found in the mud in the bottom of dry waterholes where they may estivate for many months until the return of the rainy season and the subsequent renewal of

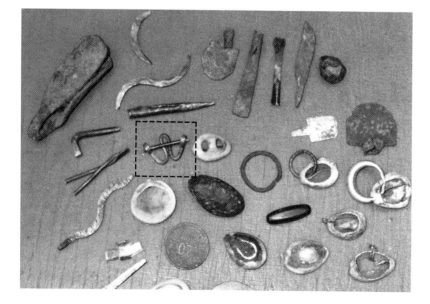

FIGURE 11. Some examples of a Sando divination kit. Each object in this set is a coded sign used by the diviner to interpret the underlying supernatural cause(s) of misfortune and to discover the correct ritual steps to be taken for healing, protection, or good fortune. The outlined object is the "manacles" sign, forged by a local blacksmith, that is part of the core divination set. Other objects, about one to two inches in length, include a red bead, a black seed, forged miniature replicas of the iron blades of key Senufo tools, and a number of cowrie shells that are marked or modified in some way to create a particular sign. Photo: Anita J. Glaze (Korhogo, March 1993).

the parched landscape. Local waterholes are usually associated both with a specific family's guardian spirits (*yirigefòlò*) and with nature spirits. The longevity and endurance of the tortoise, combined with its association with cyclical renewal and regeneration, are familiar attributes to the Senufo. Even the rounded contours of the tortoise recall the sacred circle, an important symbol of God in Senufo divination painting and a design of central importance in many areas of the arts and in rituals. Moreover, the tortoise is an icon of ideal "cool." According to my research assistants, even the land tortoises prefer the cool, moist glades that may occasionally be found within dry tracts of savannah. Finally, water is associated with the ideal state of *nyinge*, meaning both "cool," literally or figuratively, and "healthy." Restoration of *nyinge* is a principal concern of those consulting diviners.

The outstretched neck of the tortoise is a common feature of the tortoise icon, and one example on a bas-relief drum actually shows two tortoises side by side, the larger with outstretched neck.[27] The image has a provocative parallel in the courtship of the common African helmeted turtle, in which the mounting male extends his neck out over the female's head, and sways back and forth while expelling water from its nostrils. Newly hatched turtles are vulnerable to the African ground hornbill, herons, and other wetland birds of prey, while the adults of some species are omnivorous hunters and are vicious when caught—a symbolic reminder to the Senufo people of contending witches, each of whom has his own knowledge and instruments. Images of a bird or serpent grabbing a tortoise abound in the imagery of Senufo bas-relief doors and drums.

Together, the crocodile and tortoise dominate the relief panel of the Art Institute's drum in terms of both scale and position. The placement of each icon in the three-dimensional composition of the whole figure demonstrates the sculptor's ingenuity. The tortoise is centered over the rear of the female figure holding the drum aloft, thereby balancing the crocodile on the opposite side, which is the only motif that completely fills the space between the upper and lower decorative borders (see fig. 10). Indeed, the artist's sense of humor is evident in his portrayal of the crocodile taking a large bite out of the scalloped decorative band. The alignment of the crocodile along the vertical axis of the seated female figure cunningly places the tapered tail, which is suggestive of an uncircumcised penis, so that it points directly toward the female sexual parts, which are subtly indicated by the stylized notched opening of the vagina and the slightly spread thighs. Both human fertility and productivity in general are thus celebrated in this sculpture.

The master sculptor of the Art Institute's drum has made a powerful visual statement evoking the ideological importance of gender complementarity in Senufo metaphysics and ritual. The "call and response" of male and female symbolism throughout the piece reflects the African love of visual puns and an approach to symbolism that delights in double entendre. If male-oriented motifs tend to dominate the iconographic program of the bas-relief panel, it is female strength and spiritual power that holds it all together. Female gender stands for support and foundation, whether as biological mother, as "Ancient Woman" who is spirit "Mother" of the Poro Society initiates who are her "children," or as spiritual mediator through the women's Sandogo Society. The caryatid drum symbolizes archetypal Woman, a female Atlas who balances with composure the world on her head.

Brancusi's *Golden Bird*:
A New Species of Modern Sculpture

MARGHERITA ANDREOTTI

Associate Editor

The Art Institute of Chicago

In 1990, the Art Institute added *Golden Bird* (pl. 1) by Constantin Brancusi, the most widely admired sculptor of our time, to an already strong collection of his works.[1] In so doing, the museum strengthened immeasurably its collection of this artist's work. *Golden Bird* fills a significant gap by representing a theme that preoccupied Brancusi more than any other in his career, resulting in a series of almost thirty *Birds*. It is also arguably one of the most beautiful works of this series. Photographed repeatedly by Brancusi before it left his studio in 1920 for the collection of the American lawyer John Quinn, *Golden Bird* was placed by the sculptor on the fine base on which it rests today in 1926 on the occasion of a major show of his works at the Brummer Gallery in New York.[2] When the exhibition traveled to the Arts Club of Chicago in 1927, the sculpture was purchased by the club, a pioneering organization largely devoted to the exhibition and support of contemporary art, where it remained until it entered the Art Institute's collection.

It will be one of the purposes of this article to take a preliminary look at the early history of this sculpture, since, surprisingly, considering Brancusi's preeminent place in twentieth-century sculpture, even the most basic circumstances surrounding this work (its date, its relation to similar works and to the base on which it stands) are often unclear. Because of *Golden Bird*'s important place within the history of America's and especially Chicago's early support for modern art, this study concludes with a survey of its early provenance and exhibition history. It is hoped that this effort will provide a useful introduction to some of the major issues affecting this sculpture and will point to avenues for further research.[3]

Even a brief description of *Golden Bird* begins to suggest the considerable complexity underlying the sculpture's apparent simplicity. A remarkable variety of materials—wood, stone, bronze—and forms—from the geometry of the base to the fluid curves of the bird—have been brought here into exquisite balance. As Brancusi himself put it, "Simplicity is complexity itself. . . .Beauty is absolute balance," and *Golden Bird* seems indeed to embody both of these concepts.[4]

From the bottom of its wooden base to the tip of the bird's open beak, *Golden Bird* rises in an accelerating rhythm of stacked elements to a height of about seven feet. Composed of two truncated, wooden pyramids, the bottom section (21⅝ x 9 x 9 in.) is a slenderer and more rectilinear version of one of the components of Brancusi's *Endless Column* (an idea the sculptor explored in a number of variations ranging in date from 1918 to 1937; see fig. 13).[5] The central element of the base, a rectangular wooden block (17¼ x 11⅝ x 11⅝ in.), overhangs the bottom section by an inch or so on all sides. Because it is over five inches taller than it is wide, the wooden block retains the upward movement established by the bottom section, despite its bulkier shape. This central element is

FIGURE I. Constantin Brancusi (French, born Romania, 1876-1957). View of the studio, c. 1920. Photo: Marielle Tabart and Isabelle Monod-Fontaine, eds., *Brancusi, Photographer* (New York, 1979), pl. 15. On the right, the Art Institute's *Golden Bird* is shown on a series of stacked elements closely resembling the base on which it stands today (with the exception of the zigzag motif traced in chalk on the wood block). The sculpture in the foreground is a bronze version of *Mlle Pogany II*, which was sold with *Golden Bird* to the lawyer John Quinn in 1920.

distinguished by the strong pattern of tree rings visible on two of its sides (pl. 1). Brancusi once described the wood of this base as "yellow," which may have referred to its original tonality.[6] The wood is now a reddish brown. Both of these wooden sections are clearly marked with Brancusi's monogram, the letters "CB" within a circle, which appear twice on the top of the middle section and once on the upper segment of the bottom section. The geometric rigor of this part of the base seems a perfect counterpoint to the buoyant shape of the bird.

The limestone section (8⅝ in.) that directly supports the bird (37¾ in.) echoes the bottom section of the wooden base, but is composed of four rather than two truncated pyramids and is of much squatter proportions. The shape of this stone section turns out, on close inspection, not to be strictly geometric. The four truncated pyramids constituting this part of the base diminish in height and overall size as they rise, so that the bottom element, consisting of one of the four truncated pyramids, is significantly larger than the top element, in part, probably, for reasons of stability.[7] From this stone pedestal rise the "incandescent curves" (to use a phrase coined by the poet Mina Loy to describe this sculpture) of the bird itself, which appears to surge upward from a small hole in the stone.[8] The narrowness of the area from which the bird rises, no more than an inch or so in diameter (3¾ in. in circumference), is one of the most dramatic features of the piece, and one that continued to challenge Brancusi in all of his subsequent *Birds*. The cross section of this narrow area is not perfectly circular but oval, flatter at the back and narrower in front, echoing the shape of the bird as a whole. Along the bottom, Brancusi signed the piece by etching his name, "C Brancusi," into the bronze. From this attenuated beginning, the sculpture swells upward toward the bird's expanding breast, reaching a maximum circumference of twenty-one inches. The taut, almost straight line established by the bird's back, which contrasts so markedly with the pronounced curve of the front, gives the form remarkable strength and force, as it moves toward the tapering neck and beak. Polished to a reflective gold, the sculpture shines forth like a beacon.

The great beauty of this piece made a strong impact on a number of early viewers, as reflected in the writings of several poets, namely, Ezra Pound and several lesser known figures such as Jeanne Robert Foster and Mina Loy. For instance, when Pound wrote in a pioneering 1921 essay on Brancusi that "The research for the aerial has produced his [Brancusi's] bird which stands unsupported on its diminished base," he was clearly referring to this piece or to the closely related *Yellow Bird* (fig. 2), at that time the most recent of Brancusi's bird sculptures. Marveling at the sheer feat this represented, he compared Brancusi's work to that of "the best jade carvers and netsuke makers [who] produce tiny objects which also maintain themselves on extremely minute foundations." Elsewhere in his essay, Pound used the *Birds* to illustrate what he described as,

[Brancusi's] maddeningly. . .difficult exploration toward getting all the forms into one form; this is as long as any Buddhist's contemplation of the universe or as any mediaeval saint's contemplation of divine love. . . .It is a search easily begun and wholly unending, and the vestiges are let us say Brancusi's *Bird*.[9]

Similarly, Jeanne Robert Foster, a writer and poet who came to know Brancusi through the collector John Quinn, her lover during these years, marveled at the power and beauty of Brancusi's latest *Birds*:

Like Picasso, who can in a very small painting of great figures give a sense of immensity, Brancusi can in his birds of marble and bronze give the sense of space or flight in the air. One would like to see his last bird [*Yellow Bird*] in its perfected form crown a tall column. He has made many birds in bronze and marble. An essay could be written on the development and evolution of Brancusi's birds. In their last forms [referring to the *Golden Bird* and *Yellow Bird*] they are sheer perfection.[10]

Finally, Mina Loy was clearly referring to the Art Institute's *Golden Bird* in the poem she published in 1922 in *Dial*.[11] She could have easily seen the sculpture in a show held that spring (March-April) in the Sculptors' Gallery in New York, if not in Quinn's own collection. In a poem that is both witty and perceptive, she referred to the bird as "the aesthetic archetype / As if / some patient peasant God / had rubbed the Alpha and Omega / of Form / into a lump of metal." She described the bird's distilled form as "A naked orientation / unwinged unplumed / —the ultimate rhythm has lopped the extremities / of crest and claw / from / the nucleus flight." She then proceeded to comment on the bird's dazzling surface in a way that clearly identifies it with the bronze version of *Golden Bird* now in the Art Institute: "An incandescent curve / licked by chromatic flames / in labyrinths of reflections / This gong / of polished hyperaesthesia / shrills with brass / as the aggressive light / strikes / its significance." She concluded by evoking not only the sculpture's visually stunning appearance, but its pure and contemplative beauty: "The immaculate / conception / of the inaudible bird / occurs / in gorgeous reticence. . . ."

The "Road to Damascus": Brancusi's Early Development

The "sheer perfection" of *Golden Bird* was the result of long and sustained effort. This process deserves to be at least briefly summarized, if we are to have a full appreciation of the significance of this sculpture, both within

FIGURE 2. Constantin Brancusi. *Yellow Bird*, 1919. Yellow marble on stone and wood base; h. 94.6 cm, without base. New Haven, Yale University Art Gallery. Bequest of Katherine S. Dreier to the Collection Société Anonyme.

Brancusi's own development and within the history of sculpture more broadly.

By the time he conceived the Art Institute's *Golden Bird*, toward the end of 1919 or beginning of 1920,[12] Brancusi was in his early forties and had been living in Paris for over ten years. Born in Romania in 1876, he had pursued years of academic training, first at the School of Arts and Crafts in Craiova and then at the School of Fine Arts in Bucharest. Early works such as the *Anatomical Model* of 1902,[13] a tour de force of realistic modeling, show that Brancusi had achieved the major goals of a traditional artistic education: a high degree of technical skill and a thorough knowledge of the human figure, which was at the time almost the exclusive subject of sculpture. It is important to remember, in fact, that sculpture, unlike painting, did not then have a tradition of art devoted to landscape or still life, and was therefore much more narrowly focused on the figure. This situation will be of some relevance when we consider the significance of Brancusi's choice of subject for his series of *Birds*.

In 1904, Brancusi set off on foot for Paris, then the artistic capital of Europe, a trip that took him almost a year. In Paris, Brancusi was exposed over the next few years to a very wide spectrum of artistic activity, from the strictly academic efforts of a sculptor such as Antonin Mercié to the avant-garde and often primitivistic work of the Fauves (Henri Matisse, André Derain, etc.),[14] but the influence that seems most apparent in his work of these early years is that of the sculptor Auguste Rodin, who was then at the peak of his fame. Brancusi apparently even worked in his studio for a while, but left after a short time, declaring, "Nothing grows in the shadow of great trees." Brancusi's *Suffering* of 1907, a bronze version of which is in the Art Institute, exemplifies, in its poignant subject and in its fluent modeling, the type of work Brancusi produced under Rodin's influence.[15]

Other works, however, show Brancusi staking out new territory and responding to the ferment of ideas he encountered in avant-garde circles. Some of these sculptures may even be considered direct challenges to Rodin. This seems particularly true of Brancusi's *Kiss* of 1907–08 (fig. 3), which is often considered his first truly innovative work. Brancusi himself once described it as his "road to Damascus,"[16] thus emphasizing its dramatic departure from what had preceded it. In this sculpture, Brancusi took a subject made famous by Rodin, whose own marble *Kiss* was completed in 1898, and recast it in a daring new way. As Sidney Geist observed, one can hardly imagine two more different treatments of the same subject than that of Rodin and Brancusi, in material, size, process, finish, and composition.[17] It is with this work that Brancusi renounced his hard-won naturalism

FIGURE 3. Constantin Brancusi. *The Kiss*, 1907–08. Stone; h. 28 cm. Muzeul de arta, Craiova, Romania. Photo: Sidney Geist.

producing sculpture. It is also a process closer to that used in much so-called primitive sculpture, in which many of these artists were interested.

Brancusi's own statements favoring "direct carving" have led scholars to conclude that his commitment to this method was, from then on, almost exclusive.[18] As Athena Tacha Spear put it, "With a few exceptions, all his bronzes after 1910 were cast from pieces originally conceived and carved in marble (or sometimes wood)."[19] This assumption has important implications for the genesis of the Art Institute's *Golden Bird*, particularly for its relationship to the closely related *Yellow Bird* (fig. 2) in marble, now at Yale University. Based on this assumption, scholars have concluded that the Art Institute's *Golden Bird* either followed *Yellow Bird* or was based on a marble version now lost.[20]

Brancusi's Series of *Birds*

In 1910, directly following the first three renditions of *The Kiss*, Brancusi began his now famous series of birds with a sculpture generally known by its Romanian title *Pasarea Maiastra* (fig. 4), which refers to the magical "Master Bird" of Romanian folklore. The initial inspiration for this subject may have come from Igor Stravinsky's ballet *The Firebird*, which was first staged at the Paris Opéra in 1910 under the direction of Sergei Diaghilev.[21] Brancusi's sculpture and Stravinsky's ballet score both refer to a basic type of folktale that appears in many countries and in many variations throughout Europe.[22] The following characteristics recur most frequently in the folk tradition and are, to different degrees, present in Brancusi's *Birds*: the bird's spectacular, generally gold plumage, its enchanting voice, and its magical powers. It is interesting to note that the element of flight so strongly emphasized in Brancusi's later versions of the subject, starting with the type represented by the Art Institute's *Golden Bird*, seems to have been primarily an outgrowth of Brancusi's own interests rather than inherent to the folktale.

Pasarea Maiastra marks the beginning of a long series of sculptures, which some years later would include the Art Institute's *Golden Bird*, all devoted to the theme of the bird. No other subject, in fact, exists in so many variations and versions in Brancusi's work or preoccupied him so much and for so long. As Brancusi put it to his friend the composer Eric Satie, "The bird has me in its charms and will not let me go."[23] Close to thirty versions of Brancusi's *Birds* have been identified, spanning the years 1910 to 1941.[24] This body of work is even larger if we include other sculptures with birds as their subjects, such as Brancusi's series of six *Roosters*, the two groups of *Penguins* (1912 and 1911–14, the latter belonging to the Art Institute), and the various versions—at

in favor of what he often described in later years as a search for the "essence" of his subject, an essence underlying or even masked by surface appearances.

In his *Kiss*, Brancusi not only rejected the naturalism of surface that characterized the sculpture of so many of his contemporaries, but also the process—modeling —by which this was achieved. In works such as *The Kiss*, he turned to direct carving (*la taille directe*) as a means of realizing his sculptures. This approach differed markedly from the method typically used at the time by Rodin and others to realize a work in a hard stone such as marble. These artists relied on skilled technicians known as *practiciens* to transfer their modeled clay originals into marble with the aid of tools such as calipers and the pointing machine. Direct carving, by contrast, implied that the sculptor had carved the work himself directly in the stone, generally without a prior model. This process was clearly more labor intensive and less forgiving than modeling in clay, in which corrections can be made quickly and easily, but it appealed to a number of artists at this time as a more "honest" way of least three—of the *Little Bird* (1925, 1928, 1929). The series of *Roosters* includes Brancusi's very last works, which date to the late 1940s and early 1950s (the artist essentially ceased working at this time because of failing health). Since Brancusi's entire body of work includes less than three hundred sculptures,[25] this series represents a very substantial proportion of his entire output. Animal sculptures, most of them birds, constitute close to one quarter of Brancusi's sculptural oeuvre.

The rich symbolism of the bird through the ages and for Brancusi personally has been extensively treated elsewhere.[26] I will dwell briefly here on an aspect that has received less attention, the significance of Brancusi's choice of subject within a sculptural tradition almost exclusively devoted to the human figure. That this represented a considerable departure for Brancusi, comparable in some respects to his more widely hailed formal innovations, can be easily appreciated if we consider that in Rodin's sculptural output, which numbers many times that of Brancusi, it is difficult to find even one sculpture with an animal as its subject, other than the occasional mythological *Faun* or *Centauress*.

One might even venture to say that Brancusi's choice of a bird in 1910 as the subject of a major sculpture, and eventually an entire series of sculptures, may have constituted a challenge to Rodin and the tradition he represented not dissimilar to that posed by his *Kiss* of two years earlier. With his *Birds*, Brancusi went a step further by challenging not only the form, as he had done with the *Kiss*, but the very subject matter of Rodin's sculpture.

Animal sculpture in the nineteenth century was largely relegated to a category of artists called *animaliers*. The most distinguished of these was Antoine Louis Barye, who nevertheless struggled "to disprove the notion that animal images belonged to the realm of mere popular art rather than to the official hierarchy of subjects."[27] Interestingly, one of Matisse's first sculptures (1899–1901) was a copy of Barye's *Jaguar Devouring a Hare*. Before Matisse, another avant-garde painter, Edgar Degas, had also turned to animals subjects, horses, in his first free-standing sculptures (1865–81). Both Matisse and Degas may have found the sculpting of animals personally liberating, as it freed them from the conventions associated with representing the human figure, but they never made this subject matter central to their art, as Brancusi did.[28]

We have to turn to other avant-garde artists and to a somewhat later period to find an interest in animal subjects more closely comparable to that of Brancusi. It was during these very years, for instance, that the young German painter Franz Marc, an associate of Wassily Kandinsky, turned to animal subjects as the exclusive focus of his paintings, in works such as *Blue Horses* of

FIGURE 4. Constantin Brancusi. *Pasarea Maiastra*, 1910–12. White marble on stone base; h. 55.9 cm, without base. New York, The Museum of Modern Art. This is the first in a long series of works by Brancusi devoted to the theme of the bird. No other subject seems to have held quite the same fascination for the sculptor. This and the almost thirty sculptures that were to follow in the series embody not only radical innovations in form, but also a major departure in subject matter from Brancusi's previous work, which, like that of Rodin, had been almost exclusively devoted to the human figure.

1911 (Walker Art Center, Minneapolis). Marc considered animals to be spiritually superior to humans. As a result, he found them to be better subjects for his paintings, works he envisioned as "symbols. . .on the altars of a future spiritual religion."[29] As Marc explained, "People with their lack of piety, especially men, never touched my true feelings. But animals with their virginal sense of life awakened all that is good in me. . . .Very early I found people to be 'ugly': animals seemed more beautiful, more pure."[30]

Although the human figure, especially in its partial form (a head, a hand, a torso), continued to be the subject of many of his works, Brancusi seems to have shared some of Marc's hostility to the human figure, especially in its traditional naturalistic incarnations, which he referred to as "sculptured corpses." One of the aphorisms Brancusi published in 1925 in *This Quarter* made this clear: "Sculptured nude bodies are uglier than toads." Like Marc, Brancusi seems to have had a special distaste for the male figure, which he once described, using a similar phrase, as being "as ugly as a frog." He certainly shared with Marc and many other avant-garde artists of those years the belief in art's spiritual mission, its capacity to function as a substitute for religion. As Brancusi put it, "Art is the one thing that can save the world. Art is the plank after the shipwreck."[31] He would actually come very close to realizing the goal of placing his works "on the altars of a future spiritual religion," as Marc had phrased it, when, in the 1930s, the sculptor discussed plans with one of his patrons for a temple of meditation that would have featured several of his birds.[32]

Brancusi's personal interest in animals seems to have been long-standing and his appreciation of them unusually rich, extending far beyond their purely physical beauty. As Carola Giedion-Welcker wrote of one of her many conversations with the artist:

From his earliest youth Brancusi had loved and observed animals. . .his first toys were carved in wood by his own hand. These were the animals that he fed and fondled each day. . . . He laid continual stress not only on the beauty of animals, but also on the moderation of their needs, compared to those of men. The animal, he used to say, has its mating season, and follows the rhythm of nature; whereas man's degeneration is evidenced by unlimited sexual activity, a readiness—Brancusi added ironically—that he shares only with the monkey.

But besides this he felt that animals also give incomparably intense manifestations of anguish. He could never forget the sound made by a toad that, immediately before it was swallowed by a snake, let out a last crying note that was like a deeply moving lamentation and appeal for help.[33]

A short story by Brancusi published in 1925 in *This Quarter* seems to support this view. Its tone is humorous, close to that of a folktale; it is set in "very, very, very

FIGURE 5. Constantin Brancusi. *Golden Bird*, c. 1920. Gelatin silver print; 22.7 x 14.7 cm. New York, The Metropolitan Museum of Art, Ford Motor Company Collection, Gift of the Ford Motor Company and John C. Waddell (1987.1100.37). This photograph of the Art Institute's *Golden Bird* was first published (together with figs. 12 and 13) in *The Little Review* 8 (Autumn 1921), pl. 17, to accompany a pioneering article on Brancusi by the poet Ezra Pound. In this and other photographs of his polished bronzes, Brancusi manipulated the lighting conditions to dazzling effect, leading one early viewer (Henri Pierre Roché) to label them "radiant photographs" ("photos radieuses"). More specifically, Man Ray recalled, "One of his golden birds had been caught with the sun's rays striking it so that a sort of aura radiated from it, giving the work an explosive character."

ancient times," when humans and beasts "understood each other."[34]

A number of Brancusi's contemporaries, some of them perhaps influenced by Brancusi's example, sculptors such as Raymond Duchamp-Villon, Jacob Epstein, and Henri Gaudier-Brzeska, all produced a significant number of sculptures devoted to animals during these years. Some of these sculptors, including Brancusi, may have been encouraged by the example of so-called primitive art, in which animal subjects play a far more prominent role than in Western sculpture.[35] All of these artists must have appreciated that animal subjects were unencumbered by the weight of tradition associated with the human figure and therefore were especially attractive vehicles for an art that sought to break new ground. By raising animal subjects to a new level of importance, these sculptors contributed significantly to broadening the range of themes, as well as forms, available to future sculptors.

The Role of *Golden Bird* within the Series

Brancusi's series of *Birds* can be broadly divided into three types according to a chronological sequence roughly corresponding to changes in title and major changes in form: first, the *Maiastra* type (see fig. 4); secondly, the *Golden Bird* type (see pl. 1), exemplified by the Art Institute's *Golden Bird*; and third, the *Bird in Space* type (see fig. 16). Brancusi himself classified the series in this way in a handwritten list probably dating to 1936. Each type includes a number of variations, which sometimes differ from each other only slightly: there are at least seven variations of the *Maiastra* type, four of the *Golden Bird* type, and at least sixteen of the *Bird in Space* type. Of the three other versions of *Golden Bird*, only *Yellow Bird* (fig. 2) is equipped with a full-scale base and thus fully comparable to the Art Institute's piece.[36]

If we compare *Golden Bird* to the type that preceded and followed it, we see that it played a pivotal role in Brancusi's move away from a descriptive, analytical approach to his subject toward a more synthetic mode of expression. Here I am deliberately avoiding the term "abstract," since Brancusi himself so disliked it and its implication that his works were removed from reality and without meaning. *Maiastra* presents a still-identifiable tail, legs, body, neck, head, and eyes. In *Golden Bird*, the sculptor abandoned any suggestion of a clear differentiation of parts in favor of a continuous surface that evokes a bird through its subtle inflections rather than representing it.

Golden Bird is also the work in which Brancusi first began to focus on what he called "the essence of flight," an aspect that clearly dominated later versions of this subject, as the bird's form became increasingly attenuated in the many versions of *Bird in Space* (see fig. 16). As

the following statement by Brancusi suggests, the idea of flight seems to have been present early on: "I wanted to show the *Maiastra* raising its head but without putting any implication of pride, haughtiness or defiance into this gesture. That was the most difficult problem and it was only after much hard work that I managed to incorporate this gesture into the motion of flight." In later years, Brancusi came to describe his entire career as an effort to realize this aim. "All my life," he said, "I have sought the essence of flight. Flight—what bliss!"[37]

Brancusi's interest in the subject of flight and his choice of highly streamlined forms for *Golden Bird* and his subsequent series of *Birds in Space* have often struck viewers as quintessentially modern. Although Brancusi was not a vocal advocate of a "machine aesthetic," he was clearly not immune to the fascination with machine forms that so strongly affected many of his contemporaries, as demonstrated by an often-cited incident at the Paris Air Show of 1912. As retold by Natalia Dumitrescu and Alexandre Istrati, two Romanian artists who befriended Brancusi toward the end of his life,

It was about this time that he [Brancusi] had the "revelation" he so often told us about. While visiting the Paris Air Show (1912) with Léger and Duchamp, he noticed a propeller. "Now that's what I call sculpture!" he exclaimed wonderstruck. "From now on sculpture must be nothing less than that."

Fernand Léger's version of the story places an even greater emphasis on the direct challenge that this experience posed for Brancusi:

Before the Great War, I went to see the Air Show with Marcel Duchamp and Brancusi. Marcel was a dry fellow who had something elusive about him. He was strolling amid the motors and the propellers, not saying a word. Then, all of a sudden, he turned to Brancusi, "It's all over for painting. Who could better the propeller? Tell me, can you do that?"[38]

Golden Bird coincides with another important development in Brancusi's thinking. As a photograph by Brancusi suggests (fig. 8), it was during work on *Golden Bird*, or directly upon its completion, that the sculptor began another important series of birds, the *Roosters*.[39] The initial stimulus for the series probably stemmed from Brancusi's patriotic response to World War I, for it is clear that he intended these sculptures to represent the Gallic Rooster, symbol of France. In a letter to Quinn of 1922, he specifically referred to his first wooden *Rooster* as "le Coq gaulois." Brancusi added, "It's a bird once again, but it won't prevent the other one from singing, which, actually, has caught the worm."[40] In this comment, Brancusi suggested, perhaps with some intentional humor, another interpretation of the *Golden Bird*'s gesture, one based on the vividly observed reality of a bird stretching its neck to swallow a worm, reminding us once again how strongly grounded in concrete observation this bird is, despite its distilled form. While the bird's song, as Brancusi suggested in his letter, remains a component of the *Golden Bird*, it is also apparent that the two birds—the *Golden Bird* and the *Gallic Rooster*—may in a sense be viewed as complimentary, the one emphasizing the aerial and the other the auditory dimensions of the bird.

Among the most widely reproduced photographs by Brancusi is a photograph of the Art Institute's *Golden Bird* (fig. 5).[41] This photograph (which must date to no later than 1920, the year *Golden Bird* left Brancusi's studio for Quinn's collection) draws attention to one of the most striking aspects of the Art Institute's piece, as well as to one of Brancusi's major contributions to modern sculpture, the unpatinated bronze surface polished to a reflective finish. This mirrorlike surface brings light, space, and the immediate environment into the work while reducing the sense of weight and mass traditionally associated with sculpture. When struck by a source of light, the reflective surface can give the illusion that the sculpture actually radiates light, an effect captured dramatically in Brancusi's photograph. As Man Ray, the artist who is generally credited with introducing Brancusi to photography, recalled upon seeing the sculptor's early photographic prints, "One of his golden birds had been caught with the sun's rays striking it so that a sort of aura radiated from it, giving the work an explosive character."[42] Other photographs by Brancusi of *Golden Bird* in a larger studio setting show a similar effect (see fig. 8).[43] Brancusi had made relatively few works in polished bronze before this. His photographs of *Golden Bird* may thus express his exhilaration at what he may have perceived as a particularly successful marriage of surface and form.[44]

The Base

The beautiful base on which the Art Institute's *Golden Bird* rests exemplifies another of Brancusi's major contributions to modern sculpture. While sculptors before him had begun to challenge traditional solutions to the base, few tackled the issue with the sustained inventiveness of Brancusi. With extraordinary ingenuity, Brancusi created, over the course of his career, a wide range of sculptural bases for his works, bases that could serve not only as supports for sculpture and as furniture in the studio, but also as sculptures in their own right. Brancusi's *Endless Column* (see fig. 13) apparently originated as a base.[45] As already noted, modified components of *Endless Column* in fact form the top and bottom elements of the base of *Golden Bird*.

Following in Rodin's footsteps, Brancusi at times even rejected the notion that a sculpture needs a base at all. "The pedestal should be part of the sculpture," he said, "otherwise one should do away with it completely."[46] As in the case of *Golden Bird*, he often developed imaginative supports for his sculptures, playing off the form, material, and surface of the base against those of the sculpture, and controlling the sculpture's height in the process. In the Art Institute's *Golden Bird*, the elongated curves of the bird are contrasted with the angular or blocky components of the base; and the reflective metal surface of the bird is played off against the matt, light-absorbing surfaces of the stone and wood. Brancusi's love of materials is particularly evident here. He is known to have collected old pieces of wood (oak, walnut, etc.), the seasoned beauty of which especially appealed to him.[47] In fashioning the central section of the base of *Golden Bird*, Brancusi clearly cut the piece of wood to center and enhance the pattern formed by the tree rings on either side of the rectangular block. In some early photographs of the sculpture, dating to the 1930s (see fig. 6), the tree rings are aligned with the front of the sculpture and stand out as a strong formal component of the piece. A photograph by Brancusi (fig. 7) shows two bases of this type (one of which is probably the base on which *Golden Bird* rests today) standing side by side in his studio. While this photograph may have been taken to send to a prospective collector such as Quinn, it also suggests Brancusi's appreciation of these bases as independent forms. The line separating sculpture from base was at times clearly a thin one.[48]

The photographs Brancusi took of *Golden Bird* in his studio show him experimenting with a variety of bases for this sculpture, one of which (fig. 1) presents essentially the same combination of elements of the base on which *Golden Bird* rests today.[49] This base, which was not purchased by John Quinn until 1922 (two years after he acquired the sculpture with another base), was the one on which Brancusi decided to exhibit *Golden Bird* in 1926 in his first major one-person show in New York at the Brummer Gallery (see figs. 10–11), an exhibition he came to the United States to install.

Earlier, in 1922, the *Golden Bird* was included in the exhibition "Contemporary French Art" at the Sculptors' Gallery in New York (see fig. 9), where it was placed on a different base, consisting of a drum (of plaster, marble, or stone) of a type that is ubiquitous in photographs of Brancusi's studio, topped by a wooden component very similar to the bottom component of the present base. As shown in old photographs of the exhibition, the Yale *Yellow Bird* was also placed on a different base from that on which it rests today. These two versions of *Golden Bird* were shown in the Sculptors' Gallery exhibition in a manner roughly comparable to that seen in several photographs Brancusi took of them

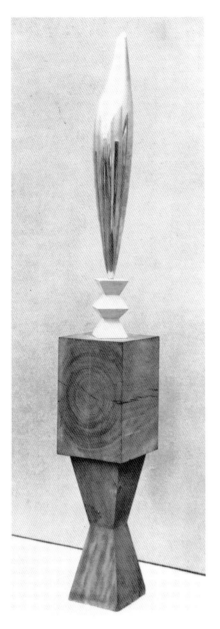

FIGURE 6. Installation of Brancusi's *Golden Bird* at the "Summer Exhibition," June 20–Aug. 20, 1934, The Renaissance Society of the University of Chicago. Photo: The Renaissance Society of the University of Chicago, *Catalogue of the Summer Exhibition* (1934), n. pag. In this and other photographs of *Golden Bird* as it was installed in the 1930s in the quarters of the Arts Club of Chicago, *Golden Bird* is shown in a slightly different relationship to its base than the one adopted in more recent installations of the piece. The tree rings that are such a striking element of the block-like component of the base were aligned then with the front rather than the side of the sculpture.

FIGURE 7. Constantin Brancusi. View of the studio with twin bases, c. 1921/22. Photo: *Brancusi, Photographer*, pl. 23.

FIGURE 8. Constantin Brancusi. Self-portrait in the studio, c. 1920. Photo: *Brancusi, Photographer*, pl. 27. In this dramatically lit photograph, the sculptor portrayed himself as mythic creator—a kind of modern Vulcan of the studio. On the left, he is shown moving a large block of marble with a crowbar. To the right of him, one can make out the tail of the unfinished *Rooster*. And on the far right is the Art Institute's *Golden Bird*, its breast glowing as the light strikes it, an effect that seems to have particularly appealed to Brancusi, since it recurs in several other photographs he took of this sculpture (see fig. 5).

in his studio (see figs. 12–13), photographs that may well have served as the basis for Quinn's original purchase of these two works.[50]

That Brancusi had no input into the installation of the sixteen works by him that were part of the Sculptors' Gallery show is known from a letter he wrote to Quinn on May 25, 1922, in which he thanked Quinn for the photographs of the exhibition but regretted its crowded installation. "What a pity that the sculptures couldn't have been placed further from the wall," he lamented. In this same letter, Brancusi mentioned that he was sending a group of numbered photographs (sixteen prints in all) of works for sale, including a group of bases. One of these, photograph number 7, is probably the photograph of twin bases mentioned above (fig. 7).[51]

The Early Collecting and Exhibition History of *Golden Bird*

Not only is *Golden Bird* a pivotal work in Brancusi's development and an outstanding sculpture in its own right, but it also occupies an important place in America's and especially Chicago's early support for modern art. As mentioned earlier, *Golden Bird* was purchased from Brancusi in 1920 by the American collector John Quinn (1870–1924). A lawyer and patron of modern writers and artists, Quinn had amassed by the time of his death in 1924 what can be fairly described as one of the first and greatest collections of modern art ever assembled.[52]

Quinn was a man of feverish energy, truly "driven," as he often described himself in his letters. He began his

FIGURE 9. Installation of "Exhibition of Contemporary French Art," Mar. 24–Apr. 10, 1922, The Sculptors' Gallery, New York. Photo: Jeanne R. Foster-William M. Murphy Collection, Rare Books and Manuscripts Division, The New York Public Library, Astor, Lenox and Tilden Foundations. The Art Institute's *Golden Bird* is the fourth sculpture from the right. The closely related *Yellow Bird* is also visible to the right of it. Both pieces are shown on different bases from those on which they rest today. This exhibition gave considerable exposure to Brancusi's work, as it included sixteen of his sculptures, but the sculptor was not at all pleased with its installation.

FIGURE 10. Yasuo Kuniyoshi (American, 1889–1953). Installation view of the Brancusi exhibition, Brummer Gallery, New York, 1926. Photo courtesy of the Photographic Archives, The Museum of Modern Art, New York. This is one of several photographs (see fig. 11) taken by the painter Kuniyoshi of what was the largest show of Brancusi's work up to that time. The Art Institute's *Golden Bird* is visible on the right.

FIGURE 11. Yasuo Kuniyoshi. Installation view of the Brancusi exhibition, Brummer Gallery, New York, 1926. Photo courtesy of the Photographic Archives, The Museum of Modern Art, New York. The drawing resting on the floor behind the sculpture on the right is now in The Art Institute of Chicago (see fig. 14). Based on this previously unpublished photograph, it can now be dated securely to no later than 1926.

collecting activity with modern literature, at one time owning the original manuscript of both James Joyce's *Ulysses* and T. S. Eliot's *Waste Land*. In 1920, he was the lawyer who defended the serialized publication of *Ulysses* in the journal *The Little Review*. Quinn was also one of the principal organizers and backers of the famous Armory Show of 1913, the first large-scale exhibition (one thousand two hundred works) of modern European and American art in the United States, which gave many Americans their first exposure to European avant-garde art. Quinn was the single biggest lender to and buyer from the Armory Show. It is here that Quinn may have received his first introduction to Brancusi's work, since the New York Armory Show included five of his sculptures, four of which were also in the smaller version of the show held later in Chicago. At his death, Quinn's collection numbered close to two thousand works. Many of the most important works in American museums today once belonged to Quinn.[53]

Quinn bought his first two sculptures by Brancusi—*Pasarea Maiastra* (fig. 4) and *Mlle Pogany* (1912, marble, Philadelphia Museum of Art)—in 1914 from Alfred Stieglitz's "291" gallery in New York. By the time of his death, ten years later, Quinn's collection of Brancusis numbered close to thirty works, including four versions of Brancusi's *Bird* and almost every major sculpture Brancusi produced during those ten years. Since Quinn did not actually meet Brancusi until his trip to Paris in 1921, he based his increasing interest in the sculptor's work on what he was able to see of his art in local exhibitions and collections, on the opinion of knowledgeable friends such as the critics Walter Pach and James Gibbons Huneker, or on that of other artists such as Jacob Epstein, as well as on photographs sent to him by Brancusi of available works. Pach actually acted as an intermediary between Brancusi and Quinn until Brancusi started corresponding directly with the collector in early 1917.[54]

By 1916, Quinn's commitment to Brancusi had grown to the point of actually commissioning a sculpture, a version of the *Kiss* in stone (Philadelphia Museum of Art), and of requesting the right of first refusal on Brancusi's next important work. In a letter to Epstein of September 8, 1916, Quinn detailed at length and with enthusiasm his acquisition of the marble *Kiss* and three wooden pieces by Brancusi: *Caryatide* (Fogg Art Museum, Harvard University, Cambridge, Mass.), a bench, and a doorway (both in the Philadelphia Museum of Art). By early 1917, Quinn had commissioned another piece, a bronze of the *Muse* (The Museum of Fine Arts, Houston). Brancusi was in fact having some difficulty by this time keeping up with Quinn's insistent requests for more works. In a letter to Quinn of June 20, 1917, he wrote, "Concerning the refusal which you have of my next important sculpture, that is understood. Only I am sorry that I cannot go quicker and that I am making you wait." Quinn also seems to have taken advantage of Brancusi's desire to concentrate his works in one collection by offering at times half, or less than half, of what Brancusi had asked for them.[55] At the same time, Quinn strenuously defended his taste for Brancusi's work to skeptics such as the painter Jack Yeats (father of the poet W. B. Yeats). In a letter of May 22, 1918, to Jack Yeats, Quinn explained, "Those Brancusi things give one a certain sense of power and have a certain explosive force. They also have a certain beauty of finish, beauty in the texture of the thing, just as many paintings have a beauty of paint, of technique, irrespective of the thing they represent." He then continued, in a more belligerent note, "The world will always be full of monstrosities like

FIGURE 12. Constantin Brancusi. View of the studio, c. 1920. Photo: Pontus Hulten, Natalia Dumitrescu, and Alexandre Istrati, *Brancusi* (New York, 1987), p. 127. Like figs. 5 and 13, this photograph of the Art Institute's *Golden Bird* and *Mlle Pogany II* was originally published in *The Little Review* 8 (Autumn 1921), pl. 24.

Rosa Bonheur's *Horse Fair* and [Emmanuel Leutze's] *Washington Crossing the Delaware* [both of which were popular works in The Metropolitan Museum of Art, New York]. To me the *Horse Fair* and *Washington Crossing the Delaware* are more monstrous than Brancusi's sculpture, and have less reason for existence."[56]

The events leading up to Quinn's purchase in November 1920 of the Art Institute's *Golden Bird*, together with *Yellow Bird* and marble and bronze versions of *Mlle Pogany II*, may be reconstructed at least tentatively, based on letters, notes, and bills quoted in a monograph on the artist by Hulten, Dumitrescu, and Istrati (see note 3 below). In January 1919, Brancusi informed Quinn that a marble *Bird* (*Maiastra*) he had offered Quinn earlier had broken during the shelling of Paris and that he would therefore not be sending it to him. According to Quinn's letter to Brancusi of October 25, 1919, the sculp-

tor went on to sell the repaired marble bird to the dealer Marius de Zayas. This reference, together with Brancusi's note of March 27, 1919, about receiving money on account from Quinn for a "*Bird*, marble, broken," suggests that Brancusi by then owed Quinn a new marble bird. On August 3, 1919, Brancusi was billed for two pieces of yellow marble, suggesting a *terminus post quem* for *Yellow Bird*, which was presumably begun to provide Quinn with the *Bird* he owed him. Brancusi exhibited *Yellow Bird* in Paris early the following year at the Salon des Indépendants (January 28–February 29, 1920). It was around this time—the end of 1919 or the beginning of 1920—that Brancusi probably cast the *Golden Bird* now in the Art Institute, a work closely related but apparently not identical to *Yellow Bird*.[57] On April 22, 1920, the writer Henri Pierre Roché asked Brancusi to send "some photographs of the bronze *Bird*" to the

FIGURE 13. Constantin Brancusi. View of the studio, c. 1920. Photo: *Brancusi, Photographer*, pl. 16. Like figs. 5 and 12, this photograph was originally published in *The Little Review* 8 (Autumn 1921), pl. 7. Among the works shown are *Yellow Bird* on the far right and the first version of *Endless Column* (1918) on the far left.

American collector Walter Arensberg. If we assume that "bronze *Bird*" refers to the Art Institute's *Golden Bird*, this letter provides a *terminus ante quem* for dating *Golden Bird*.[58] Photographs of *Golden Bird*, *Yellow Bird*, and marble and bronze versions of *Mlle Pogany II* were sent to Quinn in early October 1920, leading to his purchase of all four works in November of that same year.[59]

In 1922, the four sculptures figured in an exhibition, referred to above, at the Sculptors' Gallery in New York, to which Quinn contributed over sixty works, including sixteen pieces by Brancusi (see fig. 9). This show thus offered the public the most extensive survey of Quinn's collection before his death. Brancusi's dissatisfaction with the installation of his works possibly contributed to his decision to come to the United States twice in 1926 to direct the installation of two subsequent shows of his work in New York: a small display of his art at the Wildenstein Gallery (February ?–March 3) and the much more extensive showing at the Brummer Gallery in November.

A group of unpublished photographs of the Brummer Gallery exhibition, which were taken by the painter Yasuo Kuniyoshi at the request of Brancusi's good friend and dealer Marcel Duchamp, show Brancusi's own installation of his works.[60] Compared to the 1922 show, in which the sculptures had been shoved against the wall in bumper-to-bumper fashion, Brancusi's installation (fig. 10) gave each work considerably more breathing room. The sculptures were positioned so that similar works in different material (the bronze and marble *Birds*, the bronze and marble *Fish*, and the bronze and marble *Heads*) echoed one another across the room. As noted earlier, in one of these photographs we see that Brancusi placed *Golden Bird* on the base on which it rests today. Interestingly, perhaps because of its position in one of the corners of the room, *Golden Bird* is oriented to face one of the corners, rather than the side, of the rectangular wood block constituting the middle element of the base.

In another view of the exhibition (fig. 11), a number of drawings are shown resting on the floor. One of these, the one partly visible behind the sculpture in the right foreground, is of particular interest, since it is a portrait of Rue Winterbotham Carpenter, who was to play a crucial role in bringing *Golden Bird* to Chicago. The drawing (fig. 14), which now belongs to the Art Institute, has been traditionally dated to 1927,[61] but can now be securely dated to no later than 1926 based on this photograph and may in fact date to even earlier, to one of Mrs. Carpenter's trips to Paris.

Member of a prominent Chicago family, Rue Winterbotham Carpenter was an accomplished artist and interior decorator, and the wife of the Chicago composer John Alden Carpenter. She is generally credited as the

FIGURE 14. Constantin Brancusi. *Portrait of Rue Carpenter*, by 1926. Black chalk on paper; 645 x 450 mm. The Art Institute of Chicago, gift of Mrs. Patrick Hill in memory of her mother, Rue Winterbotham Carpenter (1981.302). Rue Winterbotham Carpenter, founder and president of The Arts Club of Chicago, was instrumental in bringing to Chicago in 1927 the largest exhibition of Brancusi's work up to that time (see figs. 15–16). The *Golden Bird* was purchased by the Arts Club from this show, where the sculpture remained, a symbol of the city's pioneering support for modern art, until it entered the Art Institute in 1990

originator of the Arts Club of Chicago, which she helped found in 1916.[62] A full decade before The Museum of Modern Art in New York was established, she apparently envisioned the Arts Club as an organization principally devoted to the exhibition and promotion of contemporary art, a role it has now fulfilled for over seventy-five years. In her capacity as president of the club (from 1918 until her death in 1931), and as a friend of Brancusi, she must have been instrumental in bringing a smaller version of the Brancusi show at the Brummer Gallery to Chicago in early 1927, thus giving the city its first extensive exposure to this artist's work.[63] She was assisted in this by Alice Roullier, a member of a family of art dealers, who

FIGURE 15. Installation view of the Brancusi exhibition, The Arts Club of Chicago, Jan. 4–22, 1927. Photo: The Arts Club Papers, The Newberry Library, Chicago. This photograph (see also fig. 16) shows Marcel Duchamp's installation of the 1927 Brancusi exhibition at the Arts Club. The Art Institute's *Golden Bird* is faintly visible in the background, where it was positioned at the entrance to the gallery.

chaired the Arts Club Exhibition Committee from 1918 to 1941. It is from this show, installed by Duchamp, that the Arts Club, in a daring gesture, bought the *Golden Bird*, a purchase that was actually destined from the beginning for the Art Institute.[64]

Several photographs of the Chicago installation of the Brancusi exhibition, which was held in the Arts Club's early quarters in the Wrigley Building, have survived (see figs. 15–16). These photographs show how Duchamp arranged the sculptures around a strong axis established by *Endless Column* and the three *Birds* included in the show (*Golden Bird*, *Bird in Space*, and *Maiastra*). In a letter to Alice Roullier of December 24, 1926, Duchamp indicated that he envisioned *Bird in Space* (see fig. 16)—then owned by photographer Edward Steichen—as one of the centerpieces of the installation.[65] Duchamp commented on this and other aspects of the exhibition in an enthusiastic letter to Brancusi of January 4, 1927:

Opening today—big success. The room [is] quite large, 13 m. by 7 m. [42½ by 23 feet], specially hung with grey canvas as [it was] at Brummer's.

Everything got here in good condition: I did my best to display things in groups.

In the middle, Steichen's *Bird*; at either end, *Golden Bird* and *Maiastra*; and, between Steichen's *Bird* and *Golden Bird*, the *Column*.

I arranged the rest around these four focal points. The effect is really satisfying; I'll send you some photos.

We may be selling *Golden Bird*, which I set at 2,000 [francs].

There has been interest in the drawings—the catalogues are selling.

All three of the *Birds* and the *Column* referred to in Duchamp's letter can be seen in one of the photographs (fig. 15). *Golden Bird* can be seen faintly glimmering in the far distance. Duchamp also preserved Brancusi's general principle of alternating sculptures in different material and size that had been carried out in the New York installation. He conveyed his final impressions of the exhibition in a letter to Brancusi on January 23:

Chicago [exhibition] over yesterday. We extended [it] four days as it was scoring, if nothing else, a moral success.

We sold *Golden Bird* to the Arts Club for 1,200 [dollars] and two drawings for 100 and 150: one to Mrs. Porter, one to Mr. Arthur Heun.

FIGURE 16. Installation view of the Brancusi exhibition, The Arts Club of Chicago, Jan. 4–22, 1927. Photo: The Arts Club Papers, The Newberry Library, Chicago. The bronze sculpture at the center is *Bird in Space* of 1925–26 (Collection of Hester Diamond), which then belonged to the photographer Edward Steichen, one of the first collectors of Brancusi's work. The piece sparked a notorious trial in 1926 when the United States Customs Office declared that it was not art but "an object of manufacture" and therefore subject to import duty. The artist eventually won the case, despite the ridicule heaped on him and his work in the press.

I'm pleased with the outcome because lots of people who liked certain things will buy in Paris.[66]

Although the Brancusi show only had a run of eighteen days in Chicago, from January 4 to 22, 1927, the response to it in the Chicago press was considerable. During a four-week period, spanning the week prior to and following the show, no less than five articles appeared on the exhibition (two in the *Chicago Illustrated News* and four in the *Chicago Evening Post*).[67] One of these, by C. J. Bulliet, a writer favorable to the artist, is worth quoting at some length, as it provides a summary of reaction to the show, as well as some insight into Duchamp's approach to Brancusi:

Brancusi's show at the Arts Club has had the expected effect on most visitors. They totally miss the point just as they always miss, and always will miss original genius—Greco, Caravaggio, Michelangelo, Ingres, Courbet, Manet, Cezanne, Matisse, Picasso, Chagall. Not since the Chagall show [held in 1926] has there been so much of outspoken protest, of suppressed sneers, of utter vacancy of expression—and not since the Chagall show has the handsome big exhibition gallery been so magnetically alive.

The individual pieces of marble, polished bronze and wood have been so arranged that the gallery as a whole gives

a first feeling of mystical wonder....Marcel Duchamp, who accompanies the Brancusi collection, as the sculptor's friend and representative, modestly disclaims any credit for the impressive arrangement of the show.

"We have only followed out Brancusi's own ideas," he says....Brancusi has in his mental and emotional make-up a strong strain of mysticism, according to Marcel Duchamp, and this mystical tendency, combined with an intellect capable of developing an idea, and a really marvelous technical skill that can visualize it, "explains" Brancusi sufficiently.[68]

Two events of these years give a further measure of the Arts Club's boldness in showing Brancusi's work and in purchasing *Golden Bird*, one of only three works apparently sold from the show. The first of these occurred in 1926. That year, the United States Customs Office decreed that *Bird in Space* (see fig. 16), upon its arrival in this country on October 1, was not art but "an object of manufacture" and therefore subject to import duty. The lengthy litigation that ensued made Brancusi's work the recipient of widespread ridicule in the press,[69] even though toward the end of 1928 a decision was handed down in the artist's favor. The second event happened in 1929. That year, the Arts Club's *Golden Bird*

FIGURE 17. Installation of Brancusi's *Golden Bird* at the "Exhibition of the School of Paris, 1910–1918," Mar. 20–Apr. 12, 1929, Harvard Society for Contemporary Art, Cambridge, Mass. Photo: *The Hound and Horn: A Harvard Miscellany* 2, 4 (July-Sept. 1929), p. 361. Newspaper reviews indicate that *Golden Bird* and the Miró painting behind it were considered the most challenging works in this exhibition, which also included tamer pieces by sculptors Aristide Maillol and Charles Despiau.

was loaned to an exhibition of recent French art held at the Harvard Society for Contemporary Art in Cambridge, Massachusetts ("An Exhibition of the School of Paris, 1910–1918," March 20–April 12).[70] Clippings of the reviews of the show were meticulously collected by its organizer, Lincoln Kirstein, in a scrapbook now in the Library of The Museum of Modern Art in New York. From these, it is evident that the Boston press singled out Brancusi's *Golden Bird*, together with a painting by Joan Miró hanging behind it, as the most difficult objects in the exhibition. Both works are shown as exhibited in a photograph reproduced in the journal *The Hound and Horn* (fig. 17).

This show, which has surprisingly gone unrecorded in the vast literature on Brancusi, included the *Golden Bird* side by side with sculptures by Charles Despiau and Aristide Maillol, sculptors who had forged their own alternatives to academic sculpture and could in a number of respects hold claim to modernity, but whose work was still entirely focused on the human figure, specifically the female nude, rendered in a simplified, yet naturalistic style. In the company of these works, Brancusi's *Golden Bird* stood out markedly: many of the reviewers could hardly make out its subject. The most sophisticated reviewer described it as "a tall object, resembling a misshapen vase, but of refined line harmony," while the less sophisticated simply made fun of it. As one of them put it, "It is safe to say there is nothing just like that bird in any ornithology in the world—headless, wingless, tailless."[71]

From the vantage point of the late twentieth century, the skepticism and ridicule that greeted Brancusi's work in the 1920s seems hard to comprehend, given the artist's current status as the most widely admired sculptor of our time. His influence has been extraordinarily wide-ranging. His most immediate impact was on sculptors such as Jean Arp, Barbara Hepworth, Henry Moore, and Isamu Noguchi, just to name a few, who appreciated the richly poetic quality of his forms. More recently, he has appealed to artists of a very different orientation, such as the Minimalists of the 1960s, who were drawn to what they saw as the rigorous abstraction of works such as *Endless Column*. Brancusi has also been an inspiration to environmental artists through his monumental complex at Tîrgu-Jiu in Romania. And some of Brancusi's sculptures, such as the Art Institute's *Golden Bird*, have indeed attained the status of "aesthetic archetype," as Mina Loy so aptly put it in 1922,[72] becoming part of a small and exclusive group of canonical works of early modern art.

PLATE 1. Constantin Brancusi (French, born Romania, 1876–1957). *Golden Bird*, 1919/20. Bronze on stone and wood base; h. 95.9 cm (37¾ in.), without base. The Art Institute of Chicago, Partial gift of the Arts Club of Chicago; restricted gift of various donors; through prior bequest of Arthur Rubloff; through prior restricted gift of William Hartmann; through prior gifts of Mr. and Mrs. Carter H. Harrison, Mr. and Mrs. Arnold H. Maremont through the Kate Maremont Foundation, Woodruff J. Parker, Mrs. Clive Runnells, Mr. and Mrs. Martin A. Ryerson, and various donors (1990.88).

PLATE 2. Japan. *Daruma*, sixteenth century.
Hanging scroll: ink and colors on silk;
109.2 x 54 cm. The Art Institute of Chicago,
Russel Tyson and Samuel M. Nickerson
endowments (1992.98).

PLATE 3. Katsushika Hokusai (Japanese, 1760–1849). *Fishing by Torchlight in Kai Province*, from the series *A Thousand Views of the Sea*, c. 1833. Woodblock print; 25.7 x 18.7 cm. The Art Institute of Chicago, Kate S. Buckingham Collection (1983.581).

PLATE 4. Katsushika Hokusai. *Chōshi in Shimōsa Province*, from the series *A Thousand Views of the Sea*, c. 1833. Woodblock print; 25.8 x 18.9 cm. The Art Institute of Chicago, Kate S. Buckingham Collection (1983.583).

PLATE 5. Katsushika Hokusai. *Whaling
off the Gotō Islands*, from the series
A Thousand Views of the Sea, c. 1833.
Woodblock print; 25.8 x 19 cm. The Art
Institute of Chicago, Kate S. Buckingham
Collection (1983.582).

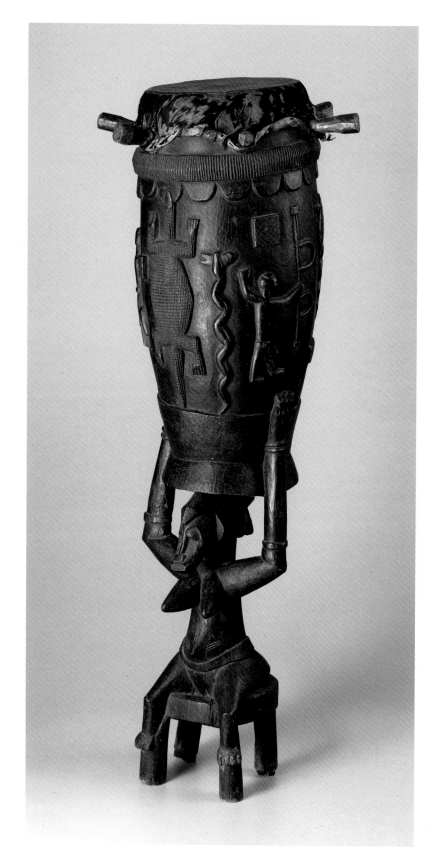

PLATE 6. Côte d'Ivoire, Senufo culture. *Female Caryatid Drum*, late nineteenth/ early twentieth century. Wood and hide; h. 123 cm, diam. at top 63.5 cm. The Art Institute of Chicago, Robert J. Hall, Herbert R. Molner Discretionary, Curator's Discretionary, and Departmental funds; Arnold Crane, Mrs. Leonard Florsheim, O. Renard Goltra, Ada Turnbull Hertle, Marion and Samuel Klasstorner, Holly and David Ross, Departmental Acquisitions endowments; through prior gifts of various donors (1990.137).

PLATE 7. Paul Strand (American, 1890–1976). *Fall in Movement*, 1973. Gelatin silver print made by Richard Benson in 1975/76 for *Portfolio Four* (16/100); 33.4 x 26.2 cm. The Art Institute of Chicago, Gift of the Paul Strand Foundation (1983.955g).

Harmonizing Form and Function: Mackay Hugh Baillie Scott and the Transformation of the Upright Piano

GHENETE ZELLEKE

Associate Curator of European Decorative Arts
The Art Institute of Chicago

Have nothing in your houses that you do not know to be useful, or believe to be beautiful.

WILLIAM MORRIS, *The Beauty of Life* (1880)

In 1985, forty years after the death of British architect and designer Mackay Hugh Baillie Scott, The Art Institute of Chicago acquired its first major example of his work and of Arts and Crafts furniture generally: an upright piano made in 1897 (pl. 8 and figs. 1–3).[1] Baillie Scott conceived of the upright piano as a horizontal cupboard or chest on a stand with two doors (fig. 1) that, when opened, reveal the keyboard (pl. 8). He transformed a monumental and almost rustic form to one of great elegance through subtle changes in proportion, bold juxtapositions of color, and sophisticated patterning. The transparent amber tones of the oak case allow the flickering grain of the wood to show through. The weight of the cupboard is supported by the piano's square-sectioned front legs, which are gradually tapered towards the top, and by the alternating ebony and oak-paneled field above the foot pedals. The top and bottom edges of the chest are outlined with a herringbone pattern in ebony and oak, while the front (fig. 1) and sides of the chest (fig. 3) are inlaid with four marquetry panels of light-colored woods, ivory, and mother-of-pearl in an ebony ground representing wild roses, flowering cherry trees, and birds. Opening the doors and raising the lid reveals additional panels of flowering cherry, apple or quince trees, and primroses that are inlaid in the doors and in the upper portion of the sloping music shelf, below which panels of golden silk are inset.[2] Scrolling copper candlesticks flank the keyboard and thick-gauge, copper mounts adorn the interior of the lid

(pl. 8 and fig. 2). The legend—John Broadwood & Sons London—is inlaid above the keyboard.

From its introduction at the Arts and Crafts exhibition in London in 1896, this novel piano form has been known as a "Manxman," after the Isle of Man home of Baillie Scott. It was created against a background of intense debate that centered on whether the musically ordained but aesthetically ungainly form of the grand and upright piano might be transformed into an object worthy of an artistic interior. During the last quarter of

PLATE 8. Mackay Hugh Baillie Scott (British, 1865-1945). *Upright or "Manxman" Piano*, 1897. Manufactured by John Broadwood and Sons, London. Oak, ebony, mother-of-pearl, ivory, copper fittings, and silk (replacement); 129.5 x 143.5 x 70 cm. The Art Institute of Chicago, Through prior restricted gifts of Robert Allerton, Margaret Day Blake, Mr. and Mrs. Leopold Blumka, Walter S. Brewster, Emily Crane Chadbourne, Richard T. Crane, Jr., Jack Linsky, Harry Manaster, Mrs. Joseph Regenstein, Sr., Mr. and Mrs. John Wilson, Mrs. Henry C. Woods; through prior acquisition of the Florene May Schoenborn and Samuel A. Marx Fund; European Decorative Arts Purchase Fund (1985.99). The design of both the grand and the upright piano was the focus of a spirited debate among British aestheticians in the last quarter of the nineteenth century. Artists and architects from Edward Burne-Jones to Baillie Scott to Charles Robert Ashbee sought to better integrate the form and decoration of the piano into contemporary, stylish interiors. Here, Baillie Scott has transformed the case of the upright piano into a garden of English pastoral delights with panels inlaid with ebony, mother-of-pearl, ivory, and various woods, mirroring the floral motifs found in his interiors.

FIGURE 1. Mackay Hugh Baillie Scott. *Upright or "Manxman" Piano* (closed view of piano in pl. 8). The form of the upright, also known as a "cottage" piano, was first developed in the early nineteenth century. In the last decade of the nineteenth century, Baillie Scott adapted the form of a cupboard for the piano, drawing the sides and lid of the piano forward to meet the pair of doors, thereby hiding the "excrescence" or projection of the keyboard. When not in use, the workings of the piano were discreetly hidden within an artistic case.

the nineteenth century, painters, architects, and designers such as Edward Burne-Jones, Lawrence Alma Tadema, Kate Faulkner for Morris and Company, and Charles Robert Ashbee experimented with the structure and surface appearance of pianos. The piano manufacturer John Broadwood and Sons was intimately involved in this transformation of the piano's exterior.

Baillie Scott's work was recognized both nationally and internationally, and was published and much discussed in the years up to World War I. He was a prolific writer, contributing from 1895 onward to *The Studio*, the London periodical that promoted contemporary artistic ideas. In his book *Houses and Gardens* (1906), he chronicled his all-encompassing ideas and designs, as well as the less than perfect reality of often "building houses for other people to furnish, or furnishing houses which other people have built."[3] That he is less well known today than William Morris, or some of his contemporaries such as Ashbee, is due in part to the destruction of a number of his most significant Arts and Crafts commissions in this period, among them the 1897/98 redecoration of the Grand Ducal Palace at Darmstadt, Germany, and a romantic tree house decorated in 1901 for Crown Princess Marie of Romania, and to the loss of many personal papers.[4] It was not until 1919 that Baillie Scott permanently moved his practice to London, his early career

having been spent on the Isle of Man (1889–1901) and in and around Bedford, near London (1901–19). His writings and his work reveal an understanding of the direction of the Arts and Crafts Movement, but the absence of personal records makes it difficult to document his contacts with contemporaries in London and elsewhere.

Mackay Hugh Baillie Scott was born in Kent on October 23, 1865, the eldest of fourteen children, to an English mother and Scottish father with extensive properties in Australia. He was sent to the Royal Agricultural College at Cirencester in preparation for managing the Australian farms, and graduated in December 1885 with a degree in drawing and science. A youthful interest in painting and drawing drew Baillie Scott instead to a career in architecture, and upon graduation he worked for Major Charles E. Davis, a Victorian architect of mediocre abilities in Bath. He remained with Davis until 1889, when he married and moved to Douglas on the Isle of Man. James D. Kornwolf, Baillie Scott's biographer, suggested that it was more than coincidence that the architect named the house he built for himself there the "Red House," echoing the name of the house Philip Webb designed for the newly married Morris in Kent, not far from London, in 1859.[5] Baillie Scott established himself as an architect in Douglas while continuing his studies in geometry and drawing at the Isle of Man School of Art.[6]

FIGURE 2. Mackay Hugh Baillie Scott. *Upright or "Manxman" Piano* (detail of interior of piano in pl. 8). Like many Arts and Crafts architects, Baillie Scott's favorite motifs were drawn from nature. The inlaid panels above the music ledge show stylized apple trees or quince trees and primroses; the stylized copper mounts on the interior of the piano's lid resemble *proteaceae*, an exotic plant native to Australia and Africa, which may have been introduced to English greenhouses.

FIGURE 3. Mackay Hugh Baillie Scott. *Upright or "Manxman" Piano* (detail of inlaid panel on side of piano in pl. 8). The briar or shrub rose with its thorny stem is evoked here in shimmering petals of mother-of-pearl and wood inlays set into the sides of the piano.

FIGURE 4. Mackay Hugh Baillie Scott. *The Studio in an Artist's House*, 1896. Photo: M. H. Baillie Scott, "An Artist's House," *The Studio* 9 (Oct. 1896), p. 31. In this barrel-vaulted interior, Baillie Scott expressed a romanticized vision of English seventeenth-century domestic life suitable for the late nineteenth century. The carved wooden wainscot and overmantle and the tall-backed armchair were inspired by traditional English models, while the chestlike form to the right resembled the newly designed cabinet of the "Manxman" piano.

FIGURE 5. Mackay Hugh Baillie Scott. *St. Mary's Home, Wantage, Berkshire*, 1898-99. Photo: Hermann Muthesius, *Das englische Haus* (1911), vol. 3, p. 119, fig. 131.

Baillie Scott took to heart the teachings of William Morris and fellow reformist John Ruskin, both of whom had set the tone for progressive discourse in the applied arts in the second half of the nineteenth century in advocating the primacy of craftsmanship both for the good of the individual and the betterment of society. In addition, by establishing Morris and Company, Morris became a moral as well as practical force in the revitalization of decorative arts, and an enormous influence on succeeding generations of British designers. Baillie Scott's goal in architecture was the realization of Ruskin's pastoral dream:

to plan and resolve to labour for the comfort and beauty of a home such as, if we could obtain it, we would quit no more . . .a cottage all of our own, with its little garden, its pleasant view, its surrounding fields, its neighbouring stream, its healthy air, and clean kitchen, parlours, and bedrooms. Less than this no man should be content with for his nest; more than this few should seek.[7]

Baillie Scott's chief architectural contribution was the reform of the small house, an area, according to Baillie Scott, hitherto ill-served by architects. Instead of following the tradition that consisted simply of scaling down the floor plan of a large house to accommodate the means of the client, Baillie Scott advocated decreasing the number of rooms for the sake of opening up larger interior spaces to serve a multitude of dining, living, and entertaining purposes. These spaces could be curtained or screened off from one another as privacy dictated. This "house which, for want of a better word, we must continue to differentiate from the ordinary house as 'artistic,' bases its claims not on its frillings and on its adornments, but on the very essence of its structure. The claims of common-sense are paramount in its plan, and its apartments are arranged to secure comfortable habitation for its inmates."[8]

Like Morris, Baillie Scott saw the home as a refuge from and an antidote to the stresses and routines of contemporary life: "On crossing the threshold we pass into a charmed territory where everything shall be in harmony."[9] He also believed that art was not set apart from but was integral to daily life: "The true place of Art is in the service of everyday life, and beautiful furniture should be found fulfilling its function in the home."[10] The design of that furniture was also the proper focus for the architect whose "conception of an interior must necessarily include the furniture which is to be used in it, and this naturally leads to the conclusion that the architect should design the chairs and tables as well as the house itself."[11] This attitude supported an anticommercial bias that Baillie Scott, like some Arts and Crafts designers, shared:

Many people appear to imagine that they cannot afford to have artistic surroundings, whereas the wonder is that they can afford so much expensive ugliness. For the vulgarity of most of the furniture of the shops has been painfully acquired at the expense of much misdirected labour.[12]

Furniture had to be practical as well as beautiful, appearing "almost to be a piece of the room in which it is placed and in absolute harmony with its surroundings."[13] The ultimate expression of this was Baillie Scott's designs for built-in furniture, such as settles or benches flanking the fireplace (see fig. 4), window seats (see fig. 5), or niches for the dining table and built-in seating.

One of the most perceptive of contemporary observers of the state of British architecture was the German architect-diplomat Hermann Muthesius. From 1896 to 1903, Muthesius was posted to the German embassy in London, where he observed the industrial and architectural achievements of Britain. In his three-volume work *Das englische Haus*, first published between 1904 and 1905, Muthesius surveyed the accomplishments of British architects and the development of the house from 1870 to 1903.[14] Baillie Scott was much admired by Muthesius for the very personal "world of fantasy and romance" he created through the use of color in his interiors:

Wooden panelling stained green in the hall and dining-room, white background colour in the drawing-room and bedrooms form the basis of the colour-scheme. Colour means everything to him, he thinks in colour from the beginning. In his simpler pieces of furniture the shade of the untreated oak is allowed to stand, others are stained more colourfully (green, red or blue) and are decorated with simple painted ornament. Yet more luxurious pieces have polychrome ornament inlaid in finely coloured woods. He likes to paint the insides of his pieces in bright colours, even—or rather, especially—when the exteriors are left plain. Baillie Scott derives his decorative motifs from plants, except when he uses a geometrical pattern for edges, etc. His furniture is always primitive or rustic in form. Yet he manages to give it a feeling of quite sophisticated intellectual culture.[15]

Morris spoke of sources of inspiration, advising "first, diligent study of Nature, and secondly, study of the work of the ages of Art. The third corrective is infallible if you have it. . .it is imagination."[16] In Baillie Scott's "world of fantasy and romance," the past and nature merged. In his sketch for the studio in an artist's house, published in *The Studio* in 1896 (fig. 4), the barrel-vaulted, barnlike interior was firmly rooted in the English vernacular. The boldly carved oak paneling over the chimney and along the walls, and the tall-backed armchair with the shaped crest rail were inspired by early seventeenth-century English models. At the far right, a portion of a chest on a stand is visible. In its overall form, hinges, and marquetry panel inlaid into the front of the door, it closely resembles the piano case at the Art Institute.

Throughout his designs for interiors, Baillie Scott's reliance on nature was evident, not only in the patterns with which the walls of his rooms were covered, but also in the motifs woven into his textiles and inlaid or painted on his furniture. The drawing room for the chaplain of St. Mary's (fig. 5) at Wantage, Berkshire, was designed in 1898. Its barrel vault was given a more sophisticated treatment than the timber frame divisions of the ceiling seen in the artist's studio (fig. 4). Indeed, the whole conception of the interior was more elegant and colorful: peacocks were painted on the fireplace wall and overgrown flowers were printed on the wallpaper. The furnishings were solidly built but exquisitely ornamented, from the long strapwork hinges terminating in stylized flowers on the cupboard or "Manxman" piano form on the left, to the tulips painted on the legs of the stool near the fireplace, and the floral upholstery of the armchair. Certain motifs recur throughout Baillie Scott's work: birds in trees or in flight; flowers such as lilies, tulips, and cultivated and wild roses; and flowering apple and cherry trees. This aesthetic, combining solid, historically resonant forms with ornament taken from nature, is apparent in his design for the upright piano.

FIGURE 6. Mackay Hugh Baillie Scott. *The "Manxman" Pianoforte*, 1896. Manufactured by John Broadwood and Sons, London. Photo: Mabel Cox, "The Arts and Crafts Exhibition," *The Artist* 18 (1896), p. 38. Baillie Scott's new design for the upright piano was first put on public display at the fifth Arts and Crafts exhibition, held in London in 1896. The piano case was made of green-stained oak and the doors were mounted with long copper straps terminating in *fleur-de-lis*. This new departure in the form of the upright was welcomed in the art press and by a portion of the musical public: at least forty pianos of this form were produced by Broadwood in the years up to 1900.

As reflected in the design literature of the last quarter of the nineteenth century, the voices of the time were raised to a sometimes comic pitch against the aesthetic shortcomings of the upright and grand pianos:

There must be some special difficulty in combining proper musical mechanism with a pleasing form, otherwise, surely, some ingenious mind would have endeavoured to benefit the shape of a grand pianoforte. As it is, it must be endured for the sake of "the soul in it, ready to waken at a touch and charm us with *invisible* beauty."[17]

Sixteen years after this lament was written, the piano could still frustrate those attempting to coordinate their interior furnishings: "The pianoforte is a bugbear to people who would fain furnish their rooms in artistic fashion."[18] The level of indignation rose to absurd levels: "The cottage piano [upright] has not been discussed here because there seems no more possibility of making it elegant than there is of making a household pet of an elephant."[19] As in so much else, Muthesius offered his own observations on the significance of the piano in the English interior:

Last of all the necessities in the drawing-room is the piano. . . .In view of the fact that the English are probably the most unmusical race in the world the presence of a grand piano in every house is slightly surprising. . .even among the educated there is a lack of critical judgment of quality in music that would be impossible in any other country.[20]

The pianomaker John Broadwood and Sons was instrumental in bringing design reform to the upright piano in the 1890s. It was a move directed as much by economics as by aesthetics. Broadwood was responding to the growing market of buyers living in apartments with rooms too small for a grand piano.[21] In 1896, Broadwood and Sons and Baillie Scott exhibited one of the most aesthetically pleasing solutions to the shape of the upright piano at the fifth Arts and Crafts Society exhibition in London (fig. 6). Since 1888, this society had sponsored exhibitions in London at annual, and later triannual, intervals. The reformist goals of this society were to provide a forum for the display of the decorative arts, to recognize the "designer and craftsman involved in its execution, as opposed to the manufacturer or middleman," to elevate public taste and "protest against ugliness [*sic*] of life," and to demonstrate that "the true root and basis of all Art lies in the handicrafts."[22]

Baillie Scott's new design, on which the Art Institute's piano is based, appeared in the exhibition's catalogue as a "Pianoforte Designed by H. B. Scott. Executed by Broadwood and Sons, with the assistance of William Hartnoll and Robert Royal. Exhibited by Broadwood and Sons."[23] A review of this exhibition in *The Artist* acknowledged that,

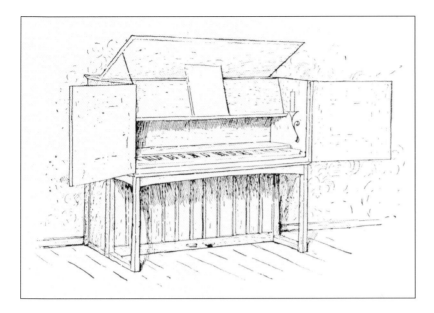

FIGURE 7. Mackay Hugh Baillie Scott. *Design for a Cottage Piano*, 1897. Photo: M. H. Baillie Scott, "On the Choice of Simple Furniture," *The Studio* 10 (Apr. 1897), p. 154.

Mr. Baillie Scott has succeeded in disguising the form of the instrument most successfully. . . by enclosing the whole thing, from the key-board upward, by means of doors. . . .The case is of green-stained oak, and is furnished with good hinges reaching almost across the doors, and lockplate and handle, all of which are in copper. . . .This is by far the best idea that has yet been reached for a cottage piano.[24]

The Cabinet Maker & Art Furnisher predicted, "There is, no doubt, much in it that will appeal to Ruskinian minds as an improvement on the current form of piano-case."[25]

In *The Studio* of April 1897, Baillie Scott published a sketch of a "cottage piano" (fig. 7) made by Broadwood and Sons that, as Baillie Scott wrote, "represents an attempt to realise something more artistic than the ordinary type of case, in which the keyboard projects as an excrescence from the main body of the piano."[26] One year later, another article appeared in *The Artist* entitled "A Treasure Chest of Tone: A Departure in the Shape of the Upright Pianoforte," in which the "Manxman" piano by Broadwood was likened to an Elizabethan "treasure chest" and illustrated by what appears to be the Art Institute's piano (fig. 8), although the notice described a green-stained instrument with "four horizontal strap-hinges. . .ending in a *fleur-de-lis device.*"[27]

This new style of upright by Baillie Scott found a market. The Broadwood records show that at least forty pianos of this form, usually identified in the Index of Uprights as "Oak Scott" or "Oak Manx," were made in the four years between January 1896, when the first "Oak Scott" piano was completed, and January 1, 1900. The firm's Day Books describe piano number 88043 as "A no. 9 Bijou Up[righ]t. P[iano]f[orte]. Oak stained green. . .after design by M.H.B.Scott Esq"; others were referred to as

"Manxman." About half of the forty pianos were left with a natural or darkened oak finish, described by the terms "unstained," "natural," "fumed," or "fumé"; the others were "stained green" or, in one instance, "stained blue." They were fitted with iron, copper, or brass hinges and straps. These pianos were sold or leased throughout Britain, and sent as far afield as Vancouver, British Columbia, and New Zealand. These "Scott" or "Manxman" uprights were put on exhibit, not only at the Arts and Crafts Society exhibition of 1896, but also later that year in Douglas on the Isle of Man as per Baillie Scott's own instructions, and in late 1900 in Liverpool for the "Grand Educational Exhibition and Sale of Work." Morris and Company hired a green stained upright with iron hinges for five days in August 1897. With two exceptions, of which the Art Institute's piano is one, all the pianos listed before 1900 were described as being unadorned except for strap hinges.[28]

The Art Institute's piano is recorded in the Index of Uprights under the serial number 89409 as an "11* Oak Manx *inlaid,*" and was finished on April 8, 1897. The virtues of this new model were advertised in Broadwood's promotional literature of 1895, "the new Upright Grand, described No. 11*. . .has attracted more attention than any other recently-made Broadwood instrument, owing, first, to its popular price and secondly to its sustaining power and beauty of tone."[29] The Art Institute's piano appears five times in the Broadwood Day Books. It was sent without charge "on hire to Messrs. H.+J. Cooper. 9 Great Pulteney St." on October 25, 1897, and returned, unsold, from Cooper's on November 13 of the same year. H. and J. Cooper was a well-known firm of "upholsterers, cabinetmakers, art decorators and designers," neigh-

THE "MANXMAN PIANOFORTE.

FIGURE 8. Mackay Hugh Baillie Scott. *The "Manxman" Pianoforte*, 1898. Manufactured by John Broadwood and Sons, London. Photo: "A Treasure Chest of Tone: A Departure in the Shape of the Upright Pianoforte," *The Artist* 21 (Jan. 1898), p. 65. The Broadwood records indicate that the Art Institute's piano was one of only two pianos richly inlaid with mother-of-pearl, ivory, and different woods designed by Baillie Scott in the years prior to 1900. Both were made in 1897; one (pl. 8) was sold in 1906 to a Mr. Ernest Harris in London; the second found an owner in New Zealand in 1902.

bors to Broadwood and Sons in London.[30] Active since at least the mid-1870s, Cooper's published *The Art of Furnishing* in 1876 and was a frequent exhibitor in international (Paris, 1878) and English exhibitions (Arts and Crafts Society exhibitions of 1889 and 1890). The firm's forte lay in exotic interiors of Arabian and Moorish inspiration and in furnishings made to their specifications in Cairo. Furniture richly inlaid with mother-of-pearl, ivory, and different woods was traditional to the Near East so it is perhaps not a coincidence that this piano was displayed at Cooper's.

The Art Institute's piano was next sent to Paterson, Sons and Company in Glasgow on November 19, 1897, where it remained unsold until returned to Broadwood's six years later on December 21, 1903, for a full credit refund of £75. Paterson, Sons and Company were piano, organ, and music sellers of Scotland since at least the 1830s, retailing British, Continental, and American pianos through their warehouse-showrooms in Edinburgh, Glasgow, Dundee, and other Scottish cities. They sold uprights and grand pianos, as well as organs, and listed Broadwood's as one of their suppliers.[31] It was another three years before the company records show that the Art Institute's piano, described as "A No. 11* Upt. Gd Pf. in dark Oak with inlaid woods and mother of pearl-design of Mr. Baillie Scott," was sold on January 18, 1906, to Ernest Harris, Esq., of 31 Lauderdale Mansions (a block of flats),

in the Maida Vale section of London for the now reduced sum of £50.[32]

This uncertain fate was also shared by a second piano designed by Baillie Scott that was finished at the same time, and sent to Cooper's for display in exchange for the Art Institute's piano, which was returned to Broadwood's. It went briefly on display in Liverpool in 1900 before its shipment in "zinc and deal" cases to a new home in New Zealand in 1902. It was described in the Day Book entry for July 26, 1902, as a "'Manxman' No. 89410 Oak case decorated with panels of inlays of coloured woods, ivory and pearl etc metal work in copper designed by H. Baillie Scott Esq." In the case of these two pianos, the records reveal the economically perilous burden assumed by Broadwood's in making such richly decorated pianos without the security of a commission from a client.

Around the time he designed the Art Institute's piano, Baillie Scott received one of his most prestigious commissions, that for the redecoration of the sitting and dining rooms of the New Palace of Ernst Ludwig, grand duke of Hesse, in Darmstadt. This commission, which included a piano (fig. 9), was undertaken between 1897 and 1898.[33] The duke of Hesse was a cultivated man and a patron of the arts who, in 1899, would establish a colony of artists at Darmstadt based on the ideals of the English Arts and Crafts Movement. Baillie Scott provided the designs for the interiors and most of the furnishings for the palace commission, which were executed by the Guild of Handicraft cabinetmakers and metalsmiths under the direction of Charles Robert Ashbee. Ashbee, a Morris disciple, established a School and Guild of Handicraft in the East End of London in 1888. His aim was "to make work of such quality as shall satisfy the demand of the professional public rather than of the Trade."[34] Baillie Scott championed the close collaboration between architect and craftsman, writing:

The designer and the workman who realises his design should bear somewhat the same relation to each other as the composer and the performer. The one interprets the ideas of the other, and in doing so adds his own personal note to the final result. . . .Most important, too, is the principle that in each piece of furniture, as far as possible, each workman shall be responsible for his own work—that there shall be as little subdivision of labour as may be, and each piece be carried through by one man.[35]

Baillie Scott noted that the duke and duchess of Hesse suggested "the general colour scheme and much of the decoration, as well as the disposition and arrangement of the furniture"[36] at Darmstadt, but an interest in bold colors and the extensive use of floral motifs were already strong currents in Baillie Scott's own approach:

FIGURE 9. Mackay Hugh Baillie Scott. *Sitting Room in the New Palace, Darmstadt, Germany, with Upright Piano*. Photo: *Möbel und Zimmereinrichtungen der Gegenwart* (Berlin, 1898), pl. 39. Baillie Scott received one of his most important commissions from Ernst Ludwig, grand duke of Hesse, who commissioned him to decorate the sitting room and dining room of the duke's New Palace at Darmstadt. While the furnishings and light fixtures were executed by Charles Robert Ashbee and the Guild of Handicraft according to Baillie Scott's designs, it is still uncertain whether the Guild decorated the upright piano, seen here in Ernst Ludwig's sitting room. The rich ornament on the piano included large pink tulips against a painted, green-toned exterior, in contrast to tulips against an orange-toned ground on the interior.

FIGURE 10. Mackay Hugh Baillie Scott. *Upright Piano*, 1902. Manufactured by John Broadwood and Sons, London. Decorated by John P. White, The Pyghtle Works, Bedford. Ebonized mahogany, pewter, ivory, mother-of-pearl, and silver-plated metal; 116.8 x 137.2 x 62.2 cm. London, Victoria and Albert Museum (W.15-1976). First shown at an exhibition of English Arts and Crafts at the Decorative Arts Museum in Budapest in 1902, this piano is the result of the collaboration between Baillie Scott and the furniture firm Pyghtle Works. The ebonized case is relieved by square panels of silvered wood and pewter carved with interwoven flowers, leaves, and branches.

In the sitting-room at Darmstadt the panelling is ivory-white, and above this the wall is orange. The central electric-light fittings, designed by Mr. Ashbee, are grey pewter, and the furniture is chiefly in tones of green and blue. And this arrangement of white, orange, grey, green and blue is supplemented by touches of brilliant pink in the flowers. In the dining-room a more sober scheme prevails, the wall above the panelling being covered with embossed leather.[37]

Many of the furnishings were of green-stained oak, inlaid with ivory and variously tinted woods, or painted in contrasting colors. Three large case pieces were made for Darmstadt: a music cabinet, a secretary, and a needlework cabinet. On their exterior, each was of green-stained oak, inlaid with long-stemmed lilies of carved ivory and various woods; their interiors were painted in white, green, and orange. In each, a relatively somber exterior concealed a bright interior, a favorite conceit of Baillie Scott's.

Baillie Scott credited an Ashbee-designed chair, exhibited at an Arts and Crafts exhibition in 1890, as inspiring an armchair with embossed leather back and a cushion of "green and blue shot Morris damask" made for Darmstadt.[38] In addition, Baillie Scott wrote that the form of a

semicircular chair (fig. 9) "was suggested by a tapestry panel by Sir Edward Burne-Jones, which was illustrated in a previous number of THE STUDIO."[39]

The most richly decorated furniture in the sitting room was a brilliantly painted piano designed by Baillie Scott (fig. 9).[40] While it no longer exists, its color is suggested by a drawing in *The Studio* in which shades of green and white on the piano's exterior are contrasted with the white, yellows, and oranges of the interior of the piano. Broadwood's was most likely responsible for the case-work of the piano, though details remain untraced in the firm's records. As the piano shares many decorative elements with the other furniture made by the Guild of Handicraft for Darmstadt, this piano may have been another collaborative effort between Baillie Scott, the Guild, and Broadwood's.

The same chestlike format that was used for the Art Institute's piano is found once more in a richly worked piano at the Victoria and Albert Museum (fig. 10). This piano is enclosed in an ebonized Cuban mahogany case inlaid with square panels of carved wood and pewter in low relief of interwoven flowers, stems, and leaves on the exterior of the doors and the sides of the piano. Structurally, this piano has a number of variations on the one in the Art Institute's collection: below the keyboard, the paneling consists of four recessed, vertical rectangular panels in ebonized wood rather than the alternation of narrow, ebony and oak panels of the Art Institute's piano; instead of being divided into three recessed panels, the sloping board above the music rest is formed as a single recessed rectangular panel.

The movement of this piano, identified by its serial number 95399, is recorded in the Broadwood Day Books. On February 11, 1902, a number 8 mahogany case (without action) was sent on hire to furnituremaker John P. White of the Pyghtle Works in Bedford.[41] With few pieces of furniture known by this firm today, the extent of Baillie Scott's collaboration with White is indicated by the catalogue *Furniture Made at the Pyghtle Works Bedford by John P. White Designed by M. H. Baillie Scott.* Published in 1901, the catalogue includes black-and-white sketches and color plates of chairs, tables, chests, cupboards, clocks, beds, and other items "made by skilled workmen under the personal supervision of the designer."[42] Baillie Scott's association with the firm went back to 1897 or 1898, and this catalogue indicates the architect's dependence on this furniture manufacturer to execute a wide range of furniture designs, as well as schemes of interior decoration including "panelling, and other fixed woodwork as well as decorative work—stencilled patterns for walls, modelled plaster, gesso work and metal work in the form of fittings for lighting, grates, &c., all classes of work in fact required for the complete furnishing and decoration of the house."[43] As

with Baillie Scott's work in general, the designs in the catalogue showed a reliance on ornament derived from flowers, including roses, lilies, daffodils, daisies, and carnations, achieved by inlaying "coloured woods with ivory, pearl, and pewter"[44] and carving in low relief.

The close correspondence of materials and decorative motifs found in some of White's furniture and in the upright piano at the Victoria and Albert Museum clearly demonstrates White's responsibility for finishing the case-work of the piano. The square panels on the sides of the piano, with stylized roses at each corner and intertwined stems that converge at the center of the panel are recurring motifs in Baillie Scott's work, as can be seen, for example, in furniture designs in White's catalogue and in other Baillie Scott interiors, as in the stenciled patterns on the wall above the fireplace in an interior of about 1906/07 (see fig. 12).

The range in price of White's work for Baillie Scott went from just over £1 to as much as £80 for the exquisitely inlaid and stained cabinet drawn in color as plate number 59. Measuring 4 feet, 9 inches in width, the cabinet was offered in oak "with inlaid decoration, in pewter, ebony, mother-of-pearl, holly, and coloured woods, and lined with brocade."[45] This cabinet was subsequently manufactured and illustrated in *The Studio* (fig. 11), its decoration in reverse of the sketch. It was described as being:

made in oak stained a dark bronze-green. On this background the stems of the roses are set and wrought in pewter, the thorns being in mother-of-pearl; and these grey stems with the blue buds, and pink roses with their grey green leaves, with touches of bright orange in the fruit of the rose, constitute the chief element in the colour-scheme. The interior is lined with syca-

FIGURE 11. Mackay Hugh Baillie Scott. *Inlaid Cabinet*, 1904. Manufactured by John P. White, The Pyghtle Works, Bedford. Oak, stained bronze-green, pewter, mother-of-pearl, sycamore, brass, and copper. Photo: "Studio-Talk," *The Studio* 32 (1904), p. 240.

more, and the parchment tints of this wood afford a well-marked contrast to the deepness of the external tones. On this light ground are pink roses and the metal-work of the handles, which are in brass and copper coloured by a special process to assume permanently prismatic tints.[46]

This lavishly ornamented cabinet and the Victoria and Albert's piano show that the Pyghtle Works was capable of working to Baillie Scott's exacting standards.[47] Other furniture of the type made by this firm are shown in an interior designed by Baillie Scott published around 1906 (fig. 12). The clock on the mantle, for example, relates to a clock illustrated as number 26 in White's catalogue. Relatively restrained in ornament, the clock is inlaid with a single bird in flight and the well-known motto "FESTINA LENTE," or "make haste slowly." An example of this clock is in the collection of the Victoria and Albert Museum.

Ashbee, Baillie Scott's collaborator at Darmstadt, also designed both grand and upright pianos for Broadwood. His first effort at piano reform was a semi-grand made as a wedding present for his wife around 1900. Rectangular in form, with long metal straps on the exterior, its interior was finely painted after his designs. The piano was a collaborative effort: Broadwood made the case; the Guild of Handicraft metalworkers made the exterior straps; and Walter Taylor, a Morris and Company employee and former Guild apprentice, painted the interior.[48] At the same time, Ashbee designed a variation on the "Manxman" upright with a pair of double-hinged doors enclosing the keyboard with metalwork executed by the Guild (fig. 13). One of several uprights of this form made by Ashbee, this

piano was executed for the industrialist E. P. Jones, and is inscribed "Designed and Ornamented by C. R. Ashbee and made by John Broadwood & Sons. . . .AD 1900."[49] Another piano of this form by Ashbee was exhibited at the 1903 Arts and Crafts exhibition, and was again a collaborative effort among Broadwood (case-work), Taylor (painted ornament), and Guild members Thornton, Downer, and Brown (ironwork).[50]

The upright pianos designed by Ashbee in the first decade of this century continued to be described as "Manxman" in the Broadwood records. In addition, simply constructed, oak or green-stained models of Baillie Scott's design were also made and sold during this period. But the overwhelming number of uprights were of conventional form, with a jutting keyboard in polished rosewood, mahogany, or walnut.

The Manxman upright piano stands as one of the most interesting expressions of English Arts and Crafts design by one of the movement's most romantic architects. Baillie Scott's close sympathy with nature can be

FIGURE 12. Mackay Hugh Baillie Scott. *Interior View*. Photo: *Deutsche Kunst und Dekoration* (1906/07), p. 429. The design of this interior shows the distance Baillie Scott had traveled in his conception of the interior. In contrast to the rustic, almost monochrome, vaulted space designed in 1896 (see fig. 4), this interior radiates a warmth and richness through intense saturations of blue, green, and orange in the furniture, much of it like that produced by The Pyghtle Works under Baillie Scott's direction, and through the treatment of the walls and floor.

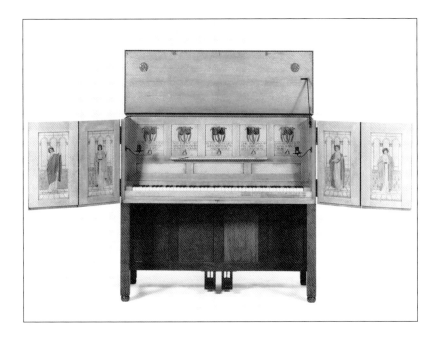

FIGURE 13. Charles Robert Ashbee (British, 1863-1942), designer. *Upright Piano*, 1900. Manufactured by John Broadwood and Sons, London. Oak, partly stained holly, pewter, and iron. Private collection.

seen not only in regularized motifs inlaid into this piano, and featured throughout his architectural interiors, but even on his tombstone, inscribed "Nature he loved, and next to Nature, Art."[51] John Broadwood and Sons led the way in reworking the form and decoration of the grand and upright pianos, commissioning architects and designers for new shapes and ornament and executing their designs. These pianos were at the forefront of artistic innovation; through exhibition and considerable press attention, they came into the public eye.

But even with the combined efforts of the venerable piano manufacturer Broadwood and distinguished designers, "artistic" pianos remained the minority taste. One critic of the time wrote, "Prominent among the artistic designers who have tackled the knotty problem of the cottage piano to some purpose, is Mr. H. Baillie Scott. The model which Mr. Baillie Scott introduced is of so revolutionary a type that it is to be feared it will be a considerable time before it achieves popularity."[52] Among the criticisms raised: "A piano ought to be unmistakably a piano; not to appear to be a cupboard nor a writing-bureau."[53] Perhaps the public shared some of Muthesius's thoughts on the attempts to make the piano artistic. While praising some of the solutions of Morris and Burne-Jones, he criticized those of "the London Arts and Crafts group" for "their rustic character. The mistake has been to consider a casing put together like a barn-door suitable to a delicate mechanism like that of the modern piano."[54] At a meeting on February 15, 1907, at the Society of Arts, an English speaker called recent attempts at reform, including that by Baillie Scott, "more eccentric and bizarre than artistic."[55]

As the Art Institute's and the Victoria and Albert's pianos indicate, lavishly decorated pianos made on speculation rather than for special commissions could be financial disasters, remaining unsold for years. George Rose, a Broadwood employee, was not unaware of the essentially conservative nature of public taste: "It was no use asking why the piano was always made of rosewood, and polished like a boot. It was simply because the public wanted it, and would not buy if it were made of anything else. . . .There is a discerning class of people, but the ordinary client would say,—'Yes, it is very nice, indeed,' but would pass good design by."[56]

A sympathetic voice in the 1880s had the foresight to predict an enduring value for artistic pianos after the initial resistance. In discussing the "exceptional merit" of an 1883 grand piano made in collaboration between John Broadwood and Sons and the artist Kate Faulkner, he wrote, "Could we look into the art museums of two or three hundred years hence, it would not surprise us to find this joint creation of musical and artistic skill surviving as a pleasing record of a somewhat restless age."[57] It has taken less than one hundred years for such creations to be recognized for their beauty and eagerly collected for future generations in public institutions in this country and abroad.

Japanese Works in The Art Institute of Chicago: Five Recent Acquisitions

JAMES T. ULAK
Associate Curator of Japanese Art
The Art Institute of Chicago

In May 1992, the galleries of East Asian art at The Art Institute of Chicago opened to the public after several years of planning and renovation. These galleries feature the museum's extensive holdings of Chinese, Japanese, and Korean art, and their configuration reflects the patterns of nearly a century of collecting. The establishment of the Department of Oriental Art in 1922 was, in fact, preceded by nearly a quarter century of astute collecting. Central to the Japanese collection was the Clarence Buckingham Collection of Japanese Woodblock Prints. Formally acquired in 1925, the collection had been housed at the Art Institute since 1914, a year after Buckingham's death. While this world-renowned collection sometimes overshadowed other aspects of the Japanese materials, a consistent pattern of acquisition in other areas of Japanese art paralleled the growth of the print collection. Through several generations, a succession of curators seemed to reach tacit accord on a philosophy of collecting. Selecting from great diversity, three specific types of art were deemed especially desirable: the woodblock print and thematically related painted images, religious iconography, and decorative painting.

In reviewing major acquisitions of Japanese art made during the past decade, it is not surprising that works in each of the categories mentioned above are most prominent. This essay examines works from all of these categories. The first of these works is a portrait of the first patriarch of Zen Buddhism, Bodhidharma, which combines appropriate psychological intensity with an opulent realism (pl. 2 and fig. 1). This sixteenth-century icon is especially striking in its affinity to warrior portraits of the period. The second work discussed is a pair of six-panel screens dating from the late seventeenth or early eighteenth century that depicts a lush cornucopia of millet under sun- and moonlight (figs. 4a-b). These screens are unique in their compositional presentation and replete with symbolic intention. The last part of the essay examines three works by the print designer and painter Katsushika Hokusai (pls. 3–5 and figs. 7–9). For nineteenth-century European and American collectors, the name Hokusai was virtually synonymous with Japanese art. His most prolific and creative period was in the 1830s, when he was in his seventies. Hokusai designed *Chie no umi,* a print series depicting the customs of fishing, for a small format, and initially ten images were produced. The extreme rarity of these prints suggests that the series was discontinued and was perhaps a commercial failure. The Art Institute was able to acquire three images from this series. They stand as a jewel-like distillation of Hokusai's haunting vision of a natural world undulating with life and as remarkable examples of the printmaker's art.

Daruma

The predominance of Japanese Buddhist iconography in the Art Institute's collection of Asian art reflects two important eras in the history of that religion. The first

FIGURE 1. Japan. *Daruma*, sixteenth century. Hanging scroll: ink and colors on silk; 109.2 x 54 cm. The Art Institute of Chicago, Russel Tyson and Samuel M. Nickerson endowments (1992.98). This icon of the patriarch Bodhidharma, while faithful to thirteenth-century prototypes, exudes a worldly vitality notable in sixteenth-century art and bears a strong resemblance to secular Japanese portraiture of the period.

era can be generally dated from the seventh century through the late twelfth century. While this era was marked by numerous stylistic changes and shifts in focus, doctrine, and patronage over the course of five centuries, the Buddhism of this period was devoted almost exclusively to the needs of the aristocracy. Indeed, there were many points when the ecclesiastical and secular authority virtually melded. The second era, which occurred in tandem with and was simultaneously stimulated by the political overthrow of the ruling Kyoto aristocracy in the late twelfth century, included a variety of populist revival movements embracing all social classes. These movements generally offered radically simplified and humanely consoling formulas for salvation. Aristocratic Buddhism relied heavily on ritual and demanded a complex iconography, reflecting a courtly manner in its measured, regal, and somewhat remote style. Populist Buddhism made as many demands on artists' workshops, although the results were more narrative in composition, evoking divine accessibility and suggesting visually the rewards of the afterlife.

Notable examples of the earlier, aristocratic Japanese Buddhist works in the Art Institute's collection include the wood and lacquer sculptures of a seated Bodhisattva and Bishamon-ten. The museum's examples of the later populist Buddhism, which are reflected mainly in the iconography of Pure Land Buddhism, include *Descent of the Amida Trinity, Seated Bodhisattva,* and *Legends of the Yūzū Nembutsu* (fig. 2), a painting that describes the origins of a proto-Pure Land Movement sect. Pure Land Buddhism was generally dismissive of esoteric approaches, and its practitioners encouraged recitation of a simple

hymn of praise: *Namu Amida Butsu,* "all praise the Lord Amida." This prayer sufficed as a means of eventual access to the Western Paradise.

Less prominently represented in the Art Institute's collection is the art of yet another revolutionary religious force: Zen Buddhism. Zen (or *Chan* in Chinese) was certainly known in Japan in the seventh century and was absorbed piecemeal by some of the established sects. It was only in the thirteenth century that the emergence of two not dissimilar political forces—one in Japan and the other in China—placed Zen in an unexpectedly dominant position in Japan. The Mongol invasions in China overwhelmed the Sung rulers by the last quarter of the thirteenth century and threatened Japan. Zen monks sought refuge under the new military government in Japan, headquartered in the tiny eastern fishing village of Kamakura. These émigré monks espoused a rigorous belief system that had emerged in sixth-century China and, in the course of time, their monasteries also became significant repositories of secular learning. In spite of frequently contentious relationships with a succession of Chinese governments, these monks were widely

FIGURE 2. Japan. *Legends of the Yūzū Nembutsu* (detail), fourteenth century. Handscroll: ink, color, and gold on paper; 30.5 x 1176.9 cm. The Art Institute of Chicago, Kate S. Buckingham Collection (1956.1256). This narrative painting describes the founding of the Yūzū sect, one of several populist Buddhist movements that preached the use of simplified salvific formulas. Seen here is Ryōnin (1073–1132), founder of the sect, receiving a vision of the Amida Buddha who affirms the correctness of the monk's teachings.

respected and influential at the highest levels of Chinese society. In return for a safe haven, they offered their Japanese protectors a style of Buddhism that matched the mood of the new regime, which was militaristic in rigor, and therefore simple and demanding. Furthermore, the émigrés offered to their hosts' nascent government a spiritually sympathetic and fully structured religious establishment. At this point, the government saw that it was possible to circumvent the symbiotic relationship between the Kyoto aristocracy and the Tendai sect, which, as the dominant esoteric sect, had a virtual monopoly over the religious beliefs of the aristocracy. Zen Buddhism, under the sponsorship of the military shogunate, would be the new government's means of regulating the often unpredictable forces of religion.[1]

The religious iconography that accompanied the Chinese monks to Japan was considerably developed. The use of imagery in the pursuit of enlightenment has always existed within Zen in a spirit of uneasy compromise. From its earliest days, Zen discouraged reliance on transmitted scripture, commentary, or image. In this way, Zen sought to redirect Buddhism to its radical and original disparagement of the senses. The senses deceive and ensnare in a cycle of desire and pain; that which is learned from the senses, or that on which the senses rely, is fundamentally suspect.

Yet, inevitably, several kinds of images enjoyed popularity. They included, most prominently, images of the Daruma and the five major patriarchs who succeeded him, images of Zen masters, images of certain trans-historical Buddhist deities particularly revered in Zen circles, images of exemplary historical and legendary figures, and nonfigural works such as landscapes or bird-and-flower paintings from which religious insight could be garnered. In some instances, the value of images was in the expression of anecdotal insight into the Zen process. The Art Institute's image of Nawa, or hemp-robed, Monju Bodhisattva (fig. 3), is typical of this approach. This image evokes the legend of a venerable Chinese scholar who was scorned for his reliance on textual learning by the Monju in the guise of a young monk. The act of composing poetry or of painting, often by amateur hands, was viewed as a tool of spiritual growth. These practices were alternatively encouraged and condemned by Zen masters. The rendering of an ink monochrome landscape became an act of reflection, a mirror of a mind's state. Within the Art Institute's collection, Sesson's *Landscape of the Four Seasons* presents a superb example of the infusion of a secular topography with religious nuance by a monk-painter.

Until recently, a credible example of patriarchal imagery from the Zen tradition was absent from the Art Institute's collection (see pl. 2 and fig. 1). Within the

FIGURE 3. Japan. *Monju in the Guise of a Hemp-Robed Youth* (*Nawa Monju*), 1415. Hanging scroll: ink and light colors on silk; 92.7 x 40.3 cm. The Art Institute of Chicago, Samuel M. Nickerson Endowment (1929.68). The deity Monju incarnated as a beautiful young monk was a popular iconographic representation in medieval Zen monasteries. According to the legend recounting his appearance, he admonishes all who are too intellectual in their pursuit of enlightenment.

FIGURE 4 a,b. Japan. *Millet Under the Aspects of Sun and Moon,* mid-seventeenth century. Pair of six-fold screens: ink, color, and gold leaf on paper; 150.4 x 349.2 cm. The Art Institute of Chicago, Restricted gift of the Rice Foundation (1989.625a-b). This stately vision of millet fields ripe for harvest is at once decorative and filled with symbolic reference. The confidence exuded in these paintings captures the mood of a country finally at peace after long political strife.

range of Zen imagery noted above, the categories of patriarch and master were perhaps the most important. The relationship between master and disciple plays a primary part in Zen Buddhism. For this reason, the image of a revered master takes logical precedence over the icon of a deity.

The semilegendary founder of Zen was Daruma (c. 470–c. 543; in Sanskrit the name is Bodhidharma), the twenty-eighth patriarch in a lineage from Sakyamini Buddha. Daruma was an Indian aristocrat who relinquished power and wealth in search of enlightenment. He journeyed to southern China and, in a cave at the Shaolin monastery, engaged in intense meditation for nine years. Daruma admonished his followers to seek single-mindedly the Buddha nature within, dispensing with a reliance on text or ritual. The emergence of Zen at this moment in Buddhism's eight-hundred-year history suggests that the reform movement was more complex than the traditional hagiography of the founder provides. The movement owes much to Buddhism's early assimilation of yogic practices in India and perhaps the melding of those practices with Taoist perspectives in China.

Images of Daruma were known in China from the eighth century onward. Essentially, three methods of pre-

senting the patriarch became standard. He was depicted full-length, standing on a reed as he coursed miraculously across the Yangzi River en route to Shaolin. He was also portrayed as seated in meditation both in a natural landscape setting, often at the mouth of a cave, or without a context. Finally, he was depicted in a three-quarter pose bust portrait, as in the Art Institute version. Inscriptions are frequently but not always in the upper portion of these works.[2]

In the Art Institute portrait (pl. 2 and fig. 1), Daruma is represented as an Indian in a rich, sensual fleshiness with full lips and a prominent nose. In this image, the patriarch's head is covered and the enveloping red robe, decorated with medallions, conceals two attributes often depicted in images of this type: earlobes elongated from the weight of earrings, which was a princely mark, and a long fingernail on the left thumb, which was the sign of an ascetic.[3] Depictions of the supposed inner state of the patriarch range from descriptive to actively engaging. The descriptive mode usually entails the seated or standing meditative figure in the context of a landscape. The viewer is invited to observe an approximation of the "historical moment" of Daruma's primary meditation experience. Noteworthy in most of these images is the depiction of the patriarch's eyes, which gaze to the far distance or are downcast, implying a reflective countenance. The mode of engagement depicts the patriarch's eyes bearing directly upon the viewer. This form is most often employed in the half-torso or bust portrait, a style that emerged no later than the early twelfth century. This style of the portrait evokes the intense connection between master and disciple, and suggests as well the

startling immediacy of enlightenment espoused by Zen. Interpretations of this gaze vary from admonitional and severe to the knowing but benevolent stare rendered in the Art Institute portrait.

Prototypes of the Daruma image certainly arrived in Japan with, if not before, the wave of Chinese immigration in the thirteenth century. For example, an ink drawing of the Six Patriarchs of the Bodhidharma Sect dated to the thirteenth century is housed at the temple Kosan-ji in Kyoto and depicts the Zen founder as a clean shaven, bald old man, Chinese in appearance and seated in a chair. This drawing is probably based on a Chinese print or book illustration of the mid-eleventh century.[4] The book is probably the earliest extant depiction of the patriarch. Several well-known early images that are also in Japanese collections depict Daruma wearing a red robe impressed with circular gold medallions, and are attributed to Chinese artists. In these examples, an Indian-featured Daruma is seated in a schematically described cave intended to represent his place of meditation at the Shaolin monastery. These paintings are among the earliest prototypes for the robe with gold emblems that were available to Japanese artists.[5] There are also other examples representing the red robe without the medallion motif.

The ink-monochrome brush of the Art Institute portrait outlines and describes a fleshy, sumptuously robed form. While these lines are deftly modulated, far more attention is paid to the face and to the pattern of the robe. The lines contain and describe a form whose central power derives not from the traditionally expected techniques of the ink-monochrome brush but from a jarring realism created by color, pattern, and enveloping

line. These features and the generally mannered sense of this portrait suggest fashionable Japanese painting of the sixteenth century. The facile combination of dexterous brush and lavish color are characteristic of a larger stylistic current which grew strong near the close of the sixteenth century. The Japanese predilection for bright, patterned forms gradually reasserted itself within structures learned from Chinese ink-monochrome and professional painting. The hand of a professional painter knowledgeable in the iconographic requirements of other Buddhist traditions and also experienced in the production of secular portraiture is apparent.[6]

Inscriptions on the reverse of the Art Institute painting indicate that it was remounted in the fourth year of Hōreki, which corresponds to the Gregorian calendar year of 1751 and that the painting was in the possession of a certain temple, Shōrin-ji. Temples generally strove to have at least important paintings remounted in one-hundred-year cycles. This general calculation allows for a mid-seventeenth century dating at the latest. But a consideration of the stylistic matters noted above comfortably places the date of execution in the mid-sixteenth century.

Millet Under the Aspects of Sun and Moon

The Art Institute's notable collection of screen paintings was enhanced with the acquisition in 1989 of an important pair of six-fold screens depicting fields of ripe millet under sun- and moonlight (figs. 4a–b). These screen paintings are striking examples of a type of painting that became increasingly prominent in the mid- to late seventeenth century.

FIGURE 5. Japan. *Maize and Cockscomb*, mid-seventeenth century. Six-fold screen: colors and gold leaf on paper; 59.4 x 169.5 cm. The Art Institute of Chicago, Kate S. Buckingham Endowment (1959.599). In the late seventeenth century, Japanese painters frequently used the large-screen format to depict flora recently imported to Japan. Maize, or corn, was one form of exotica that they chose to paint.

This pair of six-panel screens presents two views of millet fields. Each field is arrayed in bouquetlike fashion in the lower foreground of the composition. Above the fields, gold-foil clouds break in stylized scallops to reveal deep blue sky and either a circular sun in gold or a moon in silver. The sun screen depicts a field of green leafed but full-headed grain. The moon screen shows a very similar but not identical clustering with the leaf and grain treated in gold hues and covered with a light ink wash. The plants are rendered in remarkable detail. The gold-foil squares that form the cloud background have been heavily restored with gold paint, and the blue pigment of the sky is comparatively garish and quite roughly applied, suggesting later repair to substantially worn or damaged upper halves of both screens. The plant renderings, on the other hand, seem intact. Fortunately, the dramatic effect of the stark juxtaposition of finely detailed foreground and nearly blank background is intact, as well.

These paintings are unsigned and of a compositional type especially popular from the second half of the seventeenth through the early eighteenth centuries. The subjects of these paintings are frequently classical (seasonal plants are in this category) and are described in bright, opaque pigment on a bare, metallic colored or actual foil ground. Often any hint of a transitional middle ground or depth perspective is eliminated. The source for this style is usually traced to Hon'ami Kōetsu (1558–1637) and Tawaraya Sōtatsu (?–1643?), who worked both independently and as collaborators in the first quarter of the seventeenth century. Later seventeenth-century screens thought to be by followers of Sōtatsu

increasingly used a compositional device that placed subject matter, particularly plant life, in the foreground of the painting.[7] Another well-known Art Institute screen, depicting maize and cockscomb, is a prominent example of this type (fig. 7). While these artists engaged in some of the century's most notably innovative creations, virtually all of the major workshops sensed the important shifts in taste and responded by adapting their respective methods.

Millet Under the Aspects of Sun and Moon (figs. 4a–b) seems to be an adaptation of the same formula by a Tosa artist. This family of artists was closely allied with the court since Heian times (794–1185). From the early thirteenth century, they began to suffer the vicissitudes of their patrons' fortunes, and were particularly eclipsed by the popularity of the Zen-inspired ink-monochrome style. The new stability of the seventeenth century and the renewed interest in court culture drew the Tosa painters at least temporarily into the mainstream. They were propelled by the obvious talents and political acumen of Tosa Mitsuoki (1617–1691), the most prominent representative of that lineage.[8]

The Tosa style was generally characterized by representational or narrative detail and a vibrant palette. A comparison of the millet screens with the plant life renderings in the maize-and-cockscomb screen (fig. 5) is instructive. The latter was rendered generally in an uncircumscribed wash which relied often on a technique that applied wet on partially dried pigment (*tarashikomi*) for stylized modeling effects. Leaves in the millet screens were executed with light outlining for definition and a false embossing technique of layered paint (*moriage*) for dimension.

Other features of the millet screens also suggest a Tosa lineage. The subject of millet was often used by the Tosa school. Usually millet fields were rendered in a narrative that included depictions of quail, sparrows, or, in one well-known instance, roosters feasting on grain within easy reach. It has been suggested that the theme was not indigenous but adapted from Chinese sources in the fifteenth or sixteenth century.[9] The Art Institute millet screens clearly break from that narrative representation.

The use of sun and moon in the millet screens was most likely derived from several influences. The earliest prototype for the sun and moon placed within a screen with an ostensibly secular subject can be found in a pair of landscape screens from the early sixteenth century belonging to the Kongō-ji temple in Wakayama Prefecture. These works, long admired for their magisterial elegance, have been used at the temple as attendant images at ordination ceremonies. In Buddhist iconographic tradition, sun and moon, the most visible of the celestial spheres, represent the cosmos over which Buddhism exercises a benevolent reign. Because the screens were long used in the Buddhist ordination ceremonies held at this Esoteric sect temple, it was assumed that the paintings were commissioned for that expressed purpose and

that the sun and moon were, in effect, purposeful inclusions with religious meaning. While there is no convincing proof for this theory, the fact that viewers have, for some centuries, presumed this intention adds an element of interpretive richness to these or any other screens employing the paired celestial symbols.[10]

A more directly traceable literary reference in the millet screens is found in the tradition of illustrating the *Tales of Ise*, a tenth-century *uta monogatari*, or collection of loosely linked prose episodes that each contain a section of verse.[11] In the twelfth of the one hundred forty-three episodes comprising the *Tales of Ise*, a young woman of Musashi (an area now in Tokyo's western suburbs) is spirited off by her lover against her family's wishes. Pursued by authorities, they hide in the tall grasses on the Musashi plain. To the west is a vast expanse and, in the far distance, Mount Fuji is visible. As the dragnet closes in on the couple and threatens to burn the grass, the woman cries out for mercy. This poignant episode, when illustrated in a narrative fashion, usually depicted figures hiding from torch-wielding henchmen. The decidedly more refined and evocative interpretation of this episode, especially in screen format, rendered a foreground of dense, tall flowering grasses on both screens, often

FIGURE 6. Japan. *Sun and Moon with Autumn Grasses*, early seventeenth century. One of a pair of folding screens: colors on paper ground; 170.2 x 192.4 cm. The Art Institute of Chicago, Samuel M. Nickerson Endowment (1936.251). Depictions of the sun and moon at the horizon line behind a field of flowering grasses were often references to literary and historical events associated with the plain of Musashi, an expanse to the west of modern-day Tokyo.

with Mount Fuji's silhouette in the far background. Visible in the grasses at the horizon line is a red sun. In some versions, a moon is depicted on the opposite screen. Yet another category of screen using these images is simply called "sun and moon with autumn grasses"; an example of this type of screen is in the Art Institute's collection (fig. 6). In neither type are figures depicted. Either of the above types, or their variants, were probable sources for works with dense, complex foregrounds and rather plain, austere backgrounds. Beyond compositional allusions, they transmitted, as well, less easily determined literary and religious references.

Another important influence on the design of the millet screens was the newly emergent scientific observation of the time. From a scientific perspective, two features are noteworthy: the successful attempt to render the contrasting light of midday and of a moonlit night, and the accuracy of the plant renderings. Both features reflect the voracious interests of educated Japanese in the late seventeenth century. Although Japan was closed to nearly all foreign contact with the institution of the *sakoku* policy in the 1630s, the authorized Dutch trading port at Deshima in Nagasaki continued as an entry way for information from the West as well as from other parts of Asia.[12] Gardens containing herbal medicines and rare imported plants were in vogue, and their depictions in ostensibly decorative painting is noted from about this period.[13]

The simple, bold design of the Art Institute screens provides both a majestic distillation of several converging traditions and a twist of easily overlooked experimentation.

Three Prints from the Series *Chie no umi* by Hokusai

As the decade of the 1830s opened, Katsushika Hokusai (1760–1849) was seventy years old, a highly regarded artist, print designer, and book illustrator who had for more than half a century imaginatively visualized the popular culture of Edo (now known as Tokyo). At a point when his achievements had already guaranteed his position in the pantheon of important nineteenth century artists, Hokusai broke new ground. During the period sometimes called his "golden decade," he transformed what had been a secondary interest for print artists—the landscape—into a vitally expressive force.

In fairly rapid succession, Hokusai produced his *Thirty-Six Views of Mount Fuji* (*Fugaku Sanjū-Rokkei*, c. 1830–32), *One Hundred Poems by One Hundred Poets, as Told by the Nurse* (*Hyakunin Isshu Uba Ga Etoki*, c. 1831), *A Tour of Japanese Waterfalls* (*Shokoku Taki Meguri*, c. 1833–34), *Eight Views of Ryūkyū* (*Ryūkyū Hakkei*, c. 1833), and *Rare Views of Famous Japanese Bridges* (*Shokoku Meikyō Kiran*, c. 1834). Some images from among these series are so well known to both the Japanese and Western eye as to be considered synonymous with the best of Japanese art. Also during this period of intense productivity came perhaps the rarest of his landscape series, *Chie no umi* (translated as *A Thousand Views of the Sea* or *The Wisdom of the Ocean*).[14]

Three complete sets of this series are known. Within that select grouping is a set referred to as the Garland series, so designated because it was auctioned at the

FIGURE 7. Katsushika Hokusai (Japanese, 1760–1849). *Fishing by Torchlight in Kai Province*, from the series *A Thousand Views of the Sea*, c. 1833. Woodblock print; 25.7 x 18.7 cm. The Art Institute of Chicago, Kate S. Buckingham Collection (1983.581). Night fishing, either from a boat or by wading in a stream, has been perennially fascinating for onlookers. Hokusai catered to this curiosity, evoking a sense of anticipation and ritual.

FIGURE 8. Katsushika Hokusai. *Chōshi in Shimōsa Province*, from the series *A Thousand Views of the Sea*, c. 1833. Woodblock print; 25.8 x 18.9 cm. The Art Institute of Chicago, Kate S. Buckingham Collection (1983.583). The image of fishermen braving the seas off Chōshi conveys the enveloping might of nature and human courage. The figure on the prow of the foreground boat seems oblivious to risk.

Garland sale in 1945.[15] The Garland series was then purchased as a unit by a private individual who held it until 1983, when it again became available at auction.[16] On that occasion, the Art Institute acquired three of the most dramatic images from the series. *Fishing by Torchlight in Kai Province* (*Kōshū hiburi*) (pl. 3 and fig. 7), *Chōshi in Shimōsa Province* (*Sōshū Chōshi*) (pl. 4 and fig. 8), and *Whaling off the Gotō Islands* (*Gotō kujira-tsugi*) (pl. 5 and fig. 9) entered the Art Institute as superb additions to an already substantial collection of Hokusai's works. The remaining seven prints were disbursed among private collectors.[17]

If its title is considered literally, the *Chie no umi* series was projected to run to one thousand prints. Only ten images, however, are known. In addition to some extant preparatory drawings for the known completed prints, an additional two preparatory drawings (*Shinagawa* and *Kazusu no ura*) exist. Printed versions of these images are not known to have been completed, but the drawings clearly suggest that the series was moving beyond the extant ten prints.[18]

Virtually all of the works in the series contain elements recognizable in other Hokusai prints. Eight of the images are set in specific provinces, seven depict particular fishing techniques, and three reveal vistas with sea-related themes but without specific mention of techniques.

The series celebrates life and its dependence on the bounties of the sea and rivers, and it had two important commercial features: it provided a landscape travelogue with an encyclopedic compilation of ocean- and freshwater-fishing techniques and, with its concentration on depicting water, it offered an opportunity to use a pigment recently imported to Japan from Europe called Prussian blue. Roger S. Keyes suggested that Prussian blue was first used in Japan in a print made in Osaka in 1825, and appeared in some designs in Edo in 1829. This deep, bright, and chemically stable blue was resilient in the presence of light and water, and it replaced the traditional organic blues produced from *ai* (polygonum tinctorium-indigo) and *aigami* (commelina communis-dayflower), which were notoriously fugitive. The novelty of Prussian blue caused it to be used in a wide variety of prints, sometimes as the only pigment in a monochromatic palette.[19]

The *Chie no umi* images were produced on a comparatively small scale. The paper is approximately one-half the size of the sheets on which most familiar eighteenth- and nineteenth-century Japanese print images were produced; this rather standard print size is called *ōban*, and it measures approximately thirty-eight by twenty-five centimeters. The individual images in the *Chie no umi* series are on a paper size called *yoko-chūban*, measuring approximately nineteen by twenty-six centimeters. It seems reasonably clear that the *yoko-chūban* images were printed in tandem on an oban-size sheet and then cut. For example, *Fishing by Torchlight in Kai Province* and *Whaling off the Gotō Islands*, two of the three prints acquired by the Art Institute, seem to have been initially printed on single sheets. In some, but not all, impressions of the *Torchlight* print, for example, a miniscule line of a tree top can be seen at the bottom of the print, as can an oversliced remainder of the tree top in the whaling print.[20] Printed signatures and seals, as well as

FIGURE 9. Katsushika Hokusai. *Whaling off the Gotō Islands,* from the series *A Thousand Views of the Sea,* c. 1833. Woodblock print; 25.8 x 19 cm. The Art Institute of Chicago, Kate S. Buckingham Collection (1983.582). This vision of a threatening, almost demonically rendered whale surfacing so close to civilization is yet another example of Hokusai's fascination with power and danger lurking beneath the calm of everyday life. Neat rows of the fleet challenge the monster.

FIGURE 10. Katsushika Hokusai. *The Great Wave off Kanagawa,* from the series *Thirty-Six Views of Mount Fuji,* c. 1831. Woodblock print; 25.4 x 37.6 cm. The Art Institute of Chicago, Clarence Buckingham Collection (1925.3245).

censor's seals, seem to exist on alternate images, lending credence to the theory that the two images were printed on a single oban sheet that was then split.

Landscape prints began to develop as an alternative to theater and courtesan prints during the late eighteenth and early nineteenth centuries. Several factors were at play in this shift of the dominant subject matter. Throughout this period, a series of government reforms attempted to alleviate real economic crises, as well as to exercise a degree of control over a potentially disruptive merchant class. In the rigid, four-tiered neo-Confucian class system imposed by the Tokugawa government, war-

riors, farmers, artisans, and merchants were ranked in descending order of importance and privilege. This structure was largely a social fiction because the key to economic power was held by the merchant (*chōnin*) class. Merchants were the principal patrons of the metropolitan pleasure quarters and theaters. In times of economic hardship, the imposition of sumptuary laws on publishers curtailed the printing of actor and courtesan prints, and limited the kinds of pigments and precious materials that could be used in the making of prints. These measures were largely symbolic gestures intended to encourage a spirit of austerity and sobriety. In 1790, a system of government censorship was instituted that, enforced with varying degrees of severity until 1874, scrutinized the material and subject matter of prints, including attempts at political satire.

The popular pleasure genres managed to survive, and often the more controversial types of prints would elude official sanctions, but government watchfulness inevitably necessitated shifts in publishing strategies. Landscape as a subject gradually filled the void and simultaneously responded to growing public interest in the world beyond the *demimonde*. As travel restrictions in the nineteenth century became less stringent, the great highways (Tōkaidō and Kisokaidō) facilitated movement from Edo to Kyoto and points in between. Religious pilgrimage was the ostensible reason for much of the travel by commoners. Print images of popular sites served both as souvenirs for travelers and as tantalizing visions of yet-to-be-seen locales.

The increase in popularity of landscape was not sudden. From the beginning of the late seventeenth century, some use of landscape, however schematic, was visible in prints. By the last quarter of the eighteenth century, landscapes were rendered with increasing care, although they often served as backdrops for the primary figure studies. Hokusai was producing prints with landscape as the central subject in the last decade of the eighteenth century.

Because of his prodigious talent and independence, Hokusai had apprenticed in and mastered a range of print formats, an experience not normally available to artists allied with highly specialized schools. His career began under the tutelage of Katsukawa Shunshō (1726–1792), master of the workshop that dominated the production of actor and theater prints during the second half of the eighteenth century. After Hokusai's separation from the Katsukawa group in the mid-1790s, he worked as a painter and an independent designer of prints, book illustrations, and *surimono*, the limited-edition prints that were used for poetry.[21] His interest in landscape became evident in this period. Along with many other early nineteenth-century artists, he experimented with what were understood to be European or Western-style landscapes. Examples were available in books and single sheets largely through intermediary adaptation or copying by the Chinese.

The three prints chosen by the Art Institute represent the most dramatic moments in the series. *Fishing by Torchlight in Kai Province* (pl. 3 and fig. 7) depicts fishermen wading into swift rapids (Kai Province is now known as Yamashina, which is to the west of Tokyo). Some hold torches to attract fish while others reach into the water to snare the catch. The sky is rendered in an unusually deep black, with specks of stars in white reserve. The immedi-

ately surrounding embankment and foliage are rendered in a yellow-orange, suggesting the glow given off from the torchlight. The landscape grows into greens and blue greens as it recedes from the center of lighted activity. The sinuously stylized rapids emerge from a horizontally flowing river at mid-distance and then turn at a ninety-degree angle to fan into vertically cascading rapids in the center of the composition. The Prussian blue is masterfully applied from deep to lighter shades as it moves from the dark distance into the lighted foreground in alternating ribbons of pale and dark blue.

In *Chōshi in Shimōsa Province* (pl. 4 and fig. 8), two fishing boats struggling in the turbulent sea off the coast of Shimosa near the fishing village of Chōshi (in present-day Chiba Prefecture) to the east of Edo is the subject for Hokusai's bravura manipulation of Prussian blue in, once again, alternating shades. The viewer is immediately reminded of Hokusai's *Great Wave off Kanagawa* (*Kanagawa oki nami ura*) from the series *Thirty-Six Views of Mount Fuji* (fig. 10).

Whaling off the Gotō Islands (pl. 5 and fig. 9) depicts a whale as it menaces a wary fleet somewhere in the Gotō Islands off Kyūshū in the far west of Japan. While it is doubtful that Hokusai ever witnessed a scene like this, other known printed images could easily have supplied him with the inspiration. The whale emerges as a true leviathan, with threatening eye and anthropomorphic qualities. Its form is the center around which blue pigment and the churning froth of varying shades are orchestrated. What appear to be vertical stains or imperfections in the upper left center of the print are actually small columns of smoke rising from fires tended on two of the boats. This detail does not appear on all of the whaling prints and suggests some experimentation with the image.[22]

In a sense, the prints in the *Chie no umi* series were an inevitable distillation of Hokusai's long experience in small-scale print design, whether in book illustration or in the more lushly developed *surimono*. With this series, he effectively blended the intimacy of scale with the power of his larger images. The rarity of extant impressions from the series has been noted by collectors since the nineteenth century.[23] The paucity of examples suggests either that the works were commercial failures or were actually produced for an initially limited audience. It has been suggested that the prints in this series have a uniformly "muddy" quality, the result of the artist intending to approximate in some way the darker features of Western oil painting. There are indeed other examples of Hokusai's involvement in such experiments.[24] Whatever the initial response to this series, its appreciation among collectors has been constant throughout the late nineteenth and twentieth centuries.

Paul Strand's *Fall in Movement*

DAVID TRAVIS

Curator of Photography

The Art Institute of Chicago

I. Golden leaf after leaf falls from the tall acacia. Summer smiles, astonished, feeble, in this dying dream of a garden.

HERMANN HESSE, "September"

What is there to say about an autumn leaf? The range of possibilities depends more on the observer than on the leaf itself. Beyond the botany, what can be said comes from a poet's realm, frequented by everyone from lyricists to the most revered tea masters of Japan. Photographers also come and go, leaving behind calendars and their private works of art. This is no surprise, since ephemeral matters are their stock in trade. Welcome or not, photographers in this realm have been its tourists long enough that there are now more color slides of leaves than poems.

What then is there to say about a photograph of an autumn leaf, especially one in black and white? Beyond some diagram of composition, the answer to this question depends on the photographer who made it. Of Paul Strand, there is a lot to say. Of the leaf centered in his 1973 *Fall in Movement* (pl. 7 and fig. 1), there is less. We can at least say that the leaf could not have dropped from one of Strand's beloved cherry trees; the shape is too much like a maple. Although many kinds of foliage can be identified through photographs, that line of inquiry only makes an inventory list. What the leaf might have meant to the photographer, who did no gardening and did not know the nomenclature of what he found within the undergrowth, is a question with a larger answer.

The still-life photographs that Strand took in his garden during the last two decades of his life are not as famous as those from his other series: his abstractions, his details of machines, his buildings and landscapes of the Southwest, his documents of Mexico, or his portraits of village life (see figs. 2–6). The reason is simply that there were never enough garden photographs in one place at one time or for very long. Perhaps Strand felt that these were part of a series that he had not completed. When they did appear, Strand, and others after him, mixed them in with his other series.[1] Only in his last years did he publish them as a limited edition portfolio, choosing just six, none of which was among his last photographs.

Paul Strand did not begin his photographic career by pursuing nature as a subject. As a native of New York's Upper West Side, he was catapulted in 1916 at the age of twenty-six into Alfred Stieglitz's elite circle of cosmopolitan artists. His candid portraits of street people and his close-ups of kitchenware or porch shadows (see fig. 2) were praised as radically inventive photographs. His close-ups were even extreme enough to satisfy an avant-garde taste for "cubistic" abstractions. In 1920 his close-ups included a rock formation and in 1922 a mullen plant.

FIGURE 1. Paul Strand (American, 1890-1976). *Fall in Movement*, 1973. Gelatin silver print made by Richard Benson in 1975/76 for *Portfolio Four* (16/100), 33.4 x 26.2 cm. The Art Institute of Chicago, Gift of the Paul Strand Foundation (1983.955g). Although the still-life photographs that Strand took in his garden in Orgeval, France, during the last decades of his life are not as famous as his other series of abstractions, his details of machines, or his portraits of village life, the Art Institute's acquisition of *Fall in Movement* adds an important example of his work to its distinguished collection of his photography and opens the door to a new appreciation of his last works.

FIGURE 2. Paul Strand. *Porch Shadows*, 1916. Platinum and silver halide print, 33.1 x 23 cm. The Art Institute of Chicago, The Alfred Stieglitz Collection (1949.885). In his close-up photographs of ordinary objects, Strand frequently concentrated on the abstract patterns he perceived, and, in so doing, he produced a number of radically inventive images for the time.

These natural designs now replaced his artificial still lifes. By 1925, he felt he could escape the city summers and not worry about losing the income that an extended vacation in the countryside of Maine would cost. There, on Georgetown Island, he became infatuated with organic design and the natural structures they revealed.

During subsequent vacations to Maine in the company of the painter John Marin and the sculptor Gaston Lachaise, Strand's summer infatuation became a near obsession.[2] Although the irises of the Lachaise garden were close at hand (fig. 7), he sought subjects that were further afield. In 1928, while photographing on a breezy shore, he made a marvelous observation. As he recalled years later, it was "a bit of invaluable knowledge good for a life time of work."[3] Strand observed that whenever the breeze abated, the twigs and shoots resumed their previous positions so exactly that if he opened the shut-

ter only during lulls his negatives would be as sharp as if no wind had pestered him at all. The technique worked, and after discovering the trick, Strand must have felt at one with both nature and his gear, as he kept a sailor's watch across the meadows for approaching puffs.

Having extracted a secret from nature, he gained a working confidence in his abilities, expanding his horizons, as well as his philosophic approach. The next summer found him on the remote Gaspé Peninsula of the province of Quebec where he took his first photographs of open expanses (see fig. 8). Life in Gaspé affected him by the clean expression of its utility. The inhabitants had built their single wood-frame houses not to escape urban stress or to test aesthetic theory; they were there as survivors of an ancestral tradition, still making their living from the sea. On this rugged coast, a new clarity began to dawn. Strand saw that life on Gaspé was not divorced from nature as it was in New York City. Nature had an immediate connection to human existence. In the 1920s, Stieglitz had already gone back to photographing nature, but with a different end in mind. In his photographs of clouds and landscapes, Stieglitz adopted a subjective approach, equating external nature with an inner spiritual condition. Strand's more objective attitude reflected nature in the external aspects of the culture it contained. Strand began to see a wholeness to recover in out-of-the-way places. Increasingly, he sought not just a surface design but larger intangibles. During the long exposures of his camera, a settled permanence, a residual core of being, became the subject of the photograph.

Strand's empirical notion of the world took priority over his subjective and intellectual self. He disciplined his work in such a way that his still lifes of natural or man-made objects bore no sentimentality, nor did they refer back to specific aesthetic theories in the overt way his earlier abstractions had. Although he was passionate about exploring the world, Strand, unlike Stieglitz, was convinced that photographs should not be primarily about the photographer. As he said later, "The thing I see is outside myself—always. I'm not trying to describe an inner state of being."[4] This attitude suited his reserved personality, which his associates more pointedly described as remote, austere, or suspended.[5]

In the 1920s, Strand concentrated on buildings, objects, and landscapes (see figs. 4, 7, and 8). When people did appear in the next decade, during his documentary work in Mexico, they were in candid street shots taken with an angled mirror hidden on his lens (see fig. 5).[6] In the late 1940s, Strand made his first direct, head-on portraits of strangers who had agreed to pose (see fig. 6). If a few of them seem as distant as tombstones, that is because Strand strove to reflect their individual stoicism and an existence independent from his own. Thus, Strand came to face, as many scientists of the period had, the paradox of an observer trying to develop a technique so objective that it eliminated not only its own character but its very presence.

II. Men come to build stately sooner than to garden finely, as if gardening were the greater perfection.
FRANCIS BACON, "On Gardens"

More than thirty-five years after taking his first natural still lifes, Strand was able to purchase a house with a garden of its own. As Strand was no ordinary photographer, his was no ordinary garden. Visitors to La Briardière, the Strands' home outside of the village of Orgeval, France, have observed that the garden was "admirably wild."[7] Stately and fine were not quite the adjectives to describe the kind of perfection that his third wife, Hazel, with instruction from her French assistant, had brought it to. At Paul's insistence, some of the garden was kept in a partial state of decay. Visitors remarked that dead tree branches were not removed until they had completely fallen, and that leaves were left wherever they landed. Shoots from the trunk of a willow tree were left untrimmed and free to follow their natural directions.[8]

Before finding this secluded property west of Paris, Strand had not actually expressed any desire to escape the life around him. He had moved to Paris in 1950 to avoid the repressive McCarthy era in the United States, and he had spent three busy years publishing a book on France and taking the photographs for one on the Italian village of Luzzara (see fig. 9).[9] By 1954, when the Strands completed the remodeling of La Briardière, it must have seemed the perfect place for their retirement. It was peaceful and close to friends, but not too distant

FIGURE 3. Paul Strand. *Film Movement, Akeley Camera, New York,* 1923. Varnished gelatin silver print, 25.5 x 20.2 cm. The Art Institute of Chicago, Ada Turnbull Hertle Fund (1980.63). In 1922, Strand acquired an Akeley motion picture camera and began to make almost scientifically exact photographs of it in close detail. This detail view captures Strand's appreciation of its metallic surface and fine-tuned mechanical elements.

FIGURE 4. Paul Strand. *Rancho de Taos Church*, 1931. Varnished gelatin silver print, 9 x 11.7 cm. The Art Institute of Chicago, Gift of Helen Harvey Mills in memory of A. James Speyer (1986.2999).

FIGURE 5. Paul Strand. *Woman and Boy, Tenancingo, Mexico*, 1933. Hand-pulled photogravure printed in 1967 for the reissue of *The Mexican Portfolio* (1940), 16.2 x 12.7 cm. The Art Institute of Chicago, Photography Purchase Fund (1971.545). In the early 1930s, Strand worked in Mexico, where he produced documentary films and candid street photographs. The latter were often done with a right-angle mirror mounted on his lens, allowing him to capture a subject ninety degrees from where his camera was pointed.

from the capital. Its garden was also Hazel's first, replete with espaliered and free-standing pear trees. In addition, it had established rose bushes laid out in rows perpendicular to the stone façade of an old fruit barn that had previously been converted to a house. A flagstone driveway from a large wooden gate and a courtyard for playing *boules* completed the entrance. The property was big enough that arrangements were made with a French couple to maintain it all.

Strand was not a man who could take the easy life for long. His energies kept pace with his ambitions, and the good health that he had enjoyed throughout his life was still abundant. He could not just sit and watch his property being tended, nor could Hazel work constantly in the garden. In quick succession, with Hazel's encouragement and planning, they shipped out year after year, taking on extended photographic projects on the Isle of South Uist in the Outer Hebrides, and in Egypt, Romania, Morocco, and Ghana.

By 1968, however, his extensive photographic trips were over. Now that he was seventy-eight and home from traveling, the garden served as his last preserve for thinking and wandering about. Sequestered within high stone walls, he was provided with a sufficient amount of domesticated nature to stimulate his imagination and test his failing eyesight and declining health. Would lugging around his heavy camera be worth the effort? Strand need not have worried, if he did. His restricted range only served to add a touch of something once avoided: an appreciation for his own personal feelings and self-reflected thoughts.

As he entered his eighties, Strand's health began to suffer, first from cataracts and finally from a debilitating bone cancer. He saw the seasonal cycles of the garden with a new urgency, and for the first time his photographs bore metaphoric titles like *The Apple That Fell, The Garden of Eden,* and *Things Past on the Way to Oblivion* (both 1973).[10] For over fifty years he had abhorred such titles, but now they were frequent: *Iris Facing Winter* (1973), *Great Vine in Death* (1973), or *Légion d'honneur des Forêts* (c. 1973).[11] If these garden photographs were to become their own special subject during Strand's last years as a photographer, perhaps he felt they needed such titles to distinguish them from commercial calendar photography. After all, every photograph he had taken was intended to bear larger meanings than what seasonal mementos could provide. More likely, such titles were meant to differentiate his sympathetic, but objective, approach from the unfelt factual renditions of others who made evidentiary and scientific records. Perhaps, though, his resistance to such titles was simply no longer necessary. Strand had kept his faith in objective observation longer than any living photographer. Now, he permitted himself to point out interpretations that he did not want to be lost, indicating that conventional subjects could still address subjects of enormous complexity.

True to an inner drive that had sustained his long career, Strand wanted to put yet another book together. One idea he considered was an old one that had occurred

FIGURE 6. Paul Strand. *Mr. Bennett, Vermont,* 1944. Gelatin silver print made by Richard Benson in 1975/76 for *Portfolio Three* (16/100), 18.5 x 22.3 cm. The Art Institute of Chicago, Gift of the Paul Strand Foundation (1983.954f).

to him sometime after the mid-1950s when he first began to photograph his garden. He had thought of calling this book "A Bouquet of France." In it, he wanted once again to link nature with culture, this time by alternating the Orgeval photographs with his portraits of French intellectuals: Sartre, Cocteau, Braque, Picasso, and Malraux, among others. But the project attracted no publishers. Now almost two decades later, he considered publishing the garden photographs by themselves.[12] This last selection would most likely be his final book. Unlike his previous publications, however, this subject was much closer to describing his own state of mind. The book itself would be an enormous change for Strand, and perhaps this was why he procrastinated. But in truth, he had other distractions. His house was full of the activities surrounding the assembly of a comprehensive exhibition of his work and the printing of four portfolios. Sadly, "The Garden Book" was beyond his strength to finish.[13] When he died in March 1976, it was left in pieces.

III.   The one red leaf, the last of its clan,
          That dances as often as dance it can.
                    SAMUEL TAYLOR COLERIDGE, "Christabel"

It is surely not a farfetched idea to suggest that by leaving "The Garden Book" unfinished Strand kept his psychological future open.[14] All of his other projects at the time were retrospective. Whether or not this was his design, the fact of the matter was that as he devoted himself to the completion of his last four portfolios, he had little energy left for "The Garden Book." In 1975, he spent some time in New York City undergoing chemotherapy. There he made a photograph of an artificial bird that he had set on the bars of a window grating. Strand entitled it *Bird at the Edge of Space*, and it seemed as if he knew he would never take another photograph. When he returned to Orgeval, he was dying.

        We can only speculate what Strand's imagination was like just before this time, that is, during the last years

FIGURE 7. Paul Strand. *Iris, Georgetown, Maine*, 1928. Gelatin silver print made by Richard Benson in 1975/76 for *Portfolio Three* (16/100), 24.2 x 19.2 cm. The Art Institute of Chicago, Gift of the Paul Strand Foundation (1983.954c). Among the natural subjects that Strand chose for his precise, objective examination were the iris leaves in the garden of Gaston Lachaise on Georgetown Island.

FIGURE 8. Paul Strand. *Fishing Village, Gulf of St. Lawrence, Gaspé*, 1929. Gelatin silver print, 9.2 x 11.7 cm. The Art Institute of Chicago, Ada Turnbull Hertle Fund (1980.69). While vacationing on the remote peninsula of Gaspé, in Quebec, Canada, Strand discovered an environment in which life was not divorced from nature. He was struck by the simplicity and utility of the wood-framed houses of the fishing villages and by the immediate connection between nature and human existence.

he was able to make photographs. We can be certain that it was pestered by more than the sea breezes of summer days in Maine. Those were problems of finding new techniques, the problems of a younger man who in the process of solving them sought his own identity. When he found his discipline, he found his identity and dedicated himself to exploring a world outside the one he was familiar with. If his imagination were now to entertain old tricks and techniques, it would not be out of the curiosity of invention but rather to add unexpected meaning.

Only after Strand had retired from his foreign travels and the garden had become his only subject, did he begin to concentrate on an inner world. Although he was not in practice, he was not without some experience in facing what he felt about himself and putting it into photographic form. Expressing a personal state of mind had surfaced once before in several portraits taken of his first wife, Rebecca (see figs. 10–11). Now he had a second, later reason to give it voice. No longer was he addressing a subject that was as distant as the hard scrabbling for life on the Outer Hebrides. Of necessity, he was limited to the very place he did his private thinking and wandering about, to an intimate part of his own life.

As with other great artists in old age, whenever Strand faced himself in his last work, his imagination was freighted with the authority of experience. By checking off each new intuition against some memory map of well-known paths and cul-de-sacs, he saved himself from the repetitions of complacency and the false starts of momentary innovation. But, after sixty years, the question was: What province could his imagination still discover?

Look at *Fall in Movement*. In it we see the well-worn metaphor of a fecund summer's end. But is that simplicity all Strand had in mind? What about the title? Turn the photograph on its side, ninety degrees in either direction. In an awkward way, the leaves still form a picture with what surrounds it, but a change more subtle than the rotation occurs. What dynamic life the single leaf within the composition had, it loses. Turn the photograph upside down and the leaf at the center appears to have been tossed in with a chaos of falling forms. The balance of the composition is not right; the leaf no longer composes the wildness around it. Yet, when properly oriented, it regains the illusion of being suspended ever so slightly above what is underneath. Although top can be confused with bottom in this photograph, Strand had not made pictures that could be turned this far for almost fifty years. Only in his early abstractions and close-ups did he deliberately turn or tilt the composition (see figs. 2, 3, and 10). And in only one known instance in 1926 did he actually turn a composition upside down.[15] But all of that occurred when he was still searching for what photography could do. Now he was an old man after a settled, serious career, and we might well wonder: What sense of finality is this that would play with such illusions? What truths are being sought out or avoided?

If we see such illusions in *Fall in Movement*, we might postulate that Strand had reached a realm beyond kitchenware, breezy shores, or village populations. This imaginary Gaspé fronted the oceanic expanse of true self-expression. But, if yet another clarity was dawning late in his career, we have only a handful of late garden photographs with which to prove it. Of all his late garden pictures, this particular photograph, with its leaf so certain of its tentative balance, entices us to make our own conjectures. Claiming it for our own imagination, we speculate that, as in Maine and on the real Gaspé, Strand made yet another marvelous observation: each illusion eventually portrays the truth it alters.

Coming upon this idea prompts us to ask if another career for Strand could have begun with this singular photograph. If so, this new career would have been based on a quest to find out whether illusion is a confusion of subjective expectations or a mechanistic part of the phenomena that accompany objective observation. Asked another way: Did one need to return to Stieglitz's approach of investing the natural with the subjective or go even further in the opposite direction? Certainly, a photographer as skilled as Strand could tentatively examine such a paradox without first altering the kind of photography that he had come to stand for. But after a few initial probes, he would be called upon to choose up sides and consider a radical change. If such were the case, this situation may have reminded him of what he faced around 1916 as he was renouncing Pictorialism for Modernism. But even if Strand had decided to change his work beyond the new titles he proposed, such a change would have been nearly impossible. As so often happens, the old photographer was ill-equipped to pursue the new idea, and not just because of age or health or even of curiosity. Taking on such a challenge after conquering the continent of objective observation would be like leaving behind all he had so firmly established. Changing now would require a completely different set of skills.

The vision and technique that Strand had so fully under his command had taken a long time to develop. His virtuosity in photography was legendary and was not something that now could be traded in for something else. Neither could he deny his lifelong habits —his slow, thick patience waiting out shifting winds and xenophobic subjects; his austere eye meticulously adjusting, measuring, and refitting the few elements he needed, reversed and upside down, in a ground-glass frame; or his judgment experimenting day after day with old photographic printing papers in conjunction with new combinations of exposure, development, and gold toning, all to produce a single, precious print.[16] He had inherited this procedure from Stieglitz. It was a craftsman's method that responded to materials as well as an intellectual approach: the "pure expression of the object," a phrase one of Stieglitz's associates, Marius de Zayas, had coined back in 1913.[17] This method and idea had started the young Strand off by providing him with a foundation for perfecting a "straight" approach to the medium. But if illusion were a path that now led *indirectly* to a truth, was his particular virtuosity the proper vehicle to get him there?

Elsewhere, many photographers and artists in the United States and Europe were beginning to deny the need for craft and virtuosity at all. They did not bear witness to an objective world or produce any precious prints. Often they did not even make the ordinary photographs they used. Disembodied images consumed their

FIGURE 9. Paul Strand. *The Lusetti Family, Luzzara, Italy*, 1953. Gelatin silver print made by Richard Benson in 1975/76 for *Portfolio Four* (25/100), 21.7 x 27.5 cm. The Art Institute of Chicago, Gift of the Paul Strand Foundation (1983.955b).

FIGURE 10. Paul Strand. *Rebecca, New York*, 1923. Platinum print, 19.4 x 24.7 cm. The Art Institute of Chicago, Ada Turnbull Hertle Fund (1980.62). This extreme close-up and the following two photographs (figs. 11 and 12) of his first wife, Rebecca Salisbury, represent Strand's investigation of portraiture and the relationship between the inner world of his subject and his own personal state of mind.

FIGURE 11. Paul Strand. *Rebecca*, c. 1931. Platinum print, 14.8 x 11.9 cm. The Art Institute of Chicago, Ada Turnbull Hertle Fund (1980.72).

thoughts, as did theories about their reproduction and dissemination. They worked easily with illusion and conception, in a way that made the once radical idea of focussing obsessively on objects seem dated if not obsolete. With these new artists, Strand was completely out of step. If Strand's work was sincere, then irony was fashion; if well founded, then fantasy was flying high. But it was not Strand's fault that he remained steadfast to his ideals. Such disjunctions have always been among the difficulties of long, active careers examined by the light of youthful innovations.

If a private garden west of Paris were not the place that could revolutionize photography, it was still a place for the imagination to spar against one's own set notion of the world. That much we must give the old Strand credit for. After all, it was his imagination and not the toil of the gardeners that found a way to tip the whole world upside down, catch it in the fall, bring it right around again, and suspend it in a single leaf.

Such an acrobatic trick seems less convincing when performed by healthy young photographers, despite whatever wit their technical tour de force may have. Something real must be at stake to postpone death by an illusion and reshape nature with a state of mind. And it is at this point that Strand demonstrates that if his last works were to be honest, he could not go on eliminating his own presence, no matter what the habits of his long career had been.

Fall In Movement is not the kind of morbid resignation indulging in pathetic self-expression that one might expect of a lesser artist. Strand still had his discipline intact. Yet, one senses that Strand was at the edge of a vast new space that looked out to a horizon on which expressions of self-consciousness awaited. Whatever the temptations might have been, Strand knew he could not quite get there except in moments stolen in his garden. After all, he was ending a career, not beginning one. He was not on the garden's endless, cyclic track of time. For him, time was finite and linear. For him, the gravity of death was real.

In one last look at *Fall In Movement*, ask yourself: Is this photograph only about the gravity of death or about the death of gravity as well? As we look, we find the old photographer acknowledging the first interpretation, then catch him musing on the second, on a possibility of pure illusion. If this light touch tries to suspend ephemeral matter from some common destiny, we realize it is because Strand himself was not ready to retire. He creates for himself his own dispensation, because age had not slowed his imagination to a halt. Although his imagination has kept pace with its season, it has also kept its distance. Renewed by the fears, as well as the hopes, it still finds large meanings in such simple things as autumn leaves.

Notes

GLAZE, "Call and Response: A Senufo Female Caryatid Drum,"
pp. 118–133.

A NOTE ON ORTHOGRAPHY: The Central Senufo language, Senari, is
a language in which word meanings are determined in part by
tonal patterns of vowel sequence (high, mid, low, glide) requiring
an international phonetic orthography that cannot be reproduced
here. Another important determinant of word meaning is the contrast between "open" and "closed" vowels, indicated here by a dot
over the "e" ("ė" pronounced as in "pet") and the "o" ("ȯ" pronounced as in "ought"). Nasalized vowels are indicated by adding
an "n" after the vowel (for example, "en"), and a glottal stop is
indicated by an apostrophe (for example, "ka'a"). Finally, the letter
"c" is pronounced as "ch," as in "cheese."

1. Unless otherwise noted, this essay is based on over six years of
field work in northern Côte d'Ivoire among Central Senufo farmer
and artisan groups, beginning in 1969 (1969–70, 1975, 1978–79,
1982, 1984, 1987, 1992, and 1993). I have worked in sixteen
different Senufo dialect areas, from the Mali border to the Dikodougou district south of Korhogo, including Senufo artisan groups such as
the blacksmiths (Fonobele) and woodcarvers (Kulebele). As part of
field research in 1992 and 1993, respondents were shown either
photocopies or actual photographs of the caryatid drum now in
The Art Institute of Chicago collection, as well as ten additional
examples of bas-relief drums. I am especially indebted to the following Senufo research assistants: Tuo Beh, senior research assistant since 1978 (Fodombele group); Zonzerege Soro (eastern Kuleo
sculptor); Gozana Soro (Cebara diviner and linguistic assistant);
Tyemogo Kone (Kadile dialect, Tingrela), Yeo Leeluru (Nafara elder,
former diviner, and Poro song master); and numerous Kulebele
elders and woodcarvers in the Boundiali and Mbengue regions. I
should note that, as a necessary measure to help protect my sources,
it is my policy to specify ethnic group and district but not the
identity of specific villages and locations of sacred objects or activities photographed in the field.

2. Kuleeo (plural, Kuleebele) is the name of the woodcarver group
in the Cebaara dialect area around Korhogo, and is standardized to
"Kulebele" or "Kuleo" in the literature. See Dolores Richter, *Art,
Economics and Change: The Kulebele of Northern Ivory Coast* (La
Jolla, Calif., 1980); and Anita J. Glaze, *Art and Death in a Senufo
Village* (Bloomington, Ind., 1981). According to Kulebele elders at
Kolia, the western Kulebele living along the Tingrela to Boundiali
axis in the Bagoe River valley call themselves either the "Kuleebele"
or "Kuliibele," and it is the eastern branch of the Kulebele centered
in the Mbengue and Korhogo regions who are sometimes called
"Daliibele" or "Daleeble," a geographic distinction first noted in
Richter (p. 14). The Kulebele are the smallest of the endogamous,
occupation-linked artisan "castes" in Senufo culture (others include
the ubiquitous Fonobele blacksmith group, the brasscasters, pot-
ters, and leatherworkers). See also Glaze, "The Senufo," in J. P.
Barbier, ed., *Art of Côte d'Ivoire* (Geneva, 1993), vol. 1, pp. 33–36.

3. In her anthropological study of the Kulebele people, Richter
(note 2) termed "precolonial" the early traditional period prior to
1950 (p. 82), which reaches back to the arrival of the Kulebele
migrations into northern Côte d'Ivoire near the end of the eigh-

teenth century. Richter's extensive genealogical documentation has
made an invaluable contribution to the reconstruction of Senufo art
history. For a summary of Kulebele migration, see esp. pp. 81–92.

4. A bas-relief door by the master sculptor Nyaamadyo Koné of
Kolia, another recent acquisition in The Art Institute of Chicago's
African collection, appeared along with the caryatid drum in the
1991 exhibition "Senufo Woman and Art: A Caryatid Drum" (see
note 10 below). A basic visual language of bas-relief motifs is common to both eastern and western Kulebele working with object
types that would appear to be more regional in distribution. For
reference to three master carvers, all associated with the Kolia
workshop, who gained high repute as sculptors of bas-relief doors,
see A. J. Glaze, "Bas-relief Door," in Werner Schmalenbach, ed.,
African Art (Munich, 1988), p. 84.

5. Interviews in 1987, 1992, and 1993 with both western and eastern
Kulebele sculptors indicated a broadly regional typological distribution for bas-relief doors with its center at Ouazumon and Kolia,
and the probability of a single eastern Kulebele workshop, as yet
unknown, as the principle source of caryatid drums. While western
Kulebele oral histories record the importance of doors in their
workshop traditions, they had no knowledge of any Bagoe River
valley sculptors carving caryatid drums. Mbengue-region Kulebele
readily affirmed that doors were traditionally carved by the
Boundiali-region western Kulebele, and two eastern Kulebele sources
asserted that the female-caryatid drum type was eastern in provenance (i.e., "toward Mbengue"). The exact provenance of the caryatid drum, the identity of its creator, workshop locale, and followers, remains unknown. A chief Kuleeo elder in the Mbenge area
said, however, that the caryatid drum type did not come from the
important eastern Kulebele centers at Bolipe and Kanonon. Local
specialization in carving specific object types is not uncommon.
Another factor to be noted is the forced resettlement of many of
the best sculptors during the first third of the century—both
Senufo territorial overlords and colonial administrators carried off
sculptors and compelled them to produce their works against their
will. Doors collected in the Korhogo area were said to be by western sculptors who were taken there by force during colonial rule or
as part of the post-colonial diaspora of Kulebele toward Korhogo
markets. However, typological distribution patterns for Senufo
sculpture in general are markedly incomplete.

6. While living in a Kasembele village not many miles from
Mbengue, University of Illinois research scholar Thomas Bassett
(Department of Geography) witnessed the use of a female caryatid
drum in a funerary context (see fig. 5). In that context at least, the
drum was struck with signal beats rather than played in a musical
style. According to Bassett, the village chief held custodianship of
the drum (personal communication, Apr. 1993). Bassett's documentation confirms the Mbengue region as the general area for our
caryatid drum type, with special reference to its southwestern borders and the Kasembele area, but, unfortunately, no information
regarding the sculptor or workshop origin of the drum was noted.
The Kulebele workshops at both Sumo, an ancient Kulebele settlement, and nearby Sienre are the most likely possibilities.

7. The drum in the National Museum of Abidjan is illustrated in
several publications written by B. Holas, including *Sculpture Senoufo*
(Abidjan, 1964), pl. 27; *Arts traditionnels* (Abidjan, 1969), pl. 35;
and *L'Art sacré senoufo* (Abidjan, 1978), pp. 288–89. In the last of
these publications, Holas noted that the caryatid figure represents
a young female initiate of the Poro Society, who has been chosen as

drum-carrier and whose moral purity has been attested to by women elders (p. 288). Figural style, composition, and iconographic detail all compare closely with the Art Institute drum, including an identical scalloped band that creates the upper border of the bas-relief panel, and the same cross-hatching of the tortoise. Minor stylistic differences in the treatment of the female figure probably reflect two different hands, the sculptor of the Art Institute drum being intimately familiar with the work of the carver of the Abidjan drum, but tending toward a slightly more naturalistic handling of body forms such as the relationship of head, neck, and breast. While it cannot absolutely be ruled out that these differences are due to changes of style in the work of one artist, a master-apprentice relationship is more likely. Older brother-younger brother (a gap of twenty years or more is not unusual when there is more than one wife), uncle-nephew, and father-son are all common workshop combinations.

8. See A. J. Glaze, "Dialectics of Gender in Senufo Masquerades," *African Arts* 19, 3 (May 1986), esp. pp. 35–39. Female figures or heads frequently occur as center crest motifs on both face masks and helmet masks used by the men's secret societies; moreover, there is a widespread use of staffs featuring female figures, including hand-held staffs carried by male escorts in initiate dress or appearing as guardian masquerades that escort and protect a helmet masquerade. In some areas, female figural staffs are placed as guardians of male-controlled shrines and altars. In such instances, the female icon serves as a powerful supernatural force that seeks out sorcery, clears the path, or acts as guardian and protector against potential threats or intrusion. The pattern is a structural duality that pairs female sculptural forms with male sacred spaces or activities. Field documentation of the above contexts indicated that these gender-linked combinations reflect the Senufo concept of the saving powers of women diviners and their special relationship with their tutelary and messenger nature spirits. See also Glaze, "Two Guardian Figure Staffs," in Barbier (note 2), vol. 2, p. 34.

9. The symbolic parallel relationship of "Ancient Woman" (*Kaceleëò*) and the oldest woman of the matrilineage is carefully articulated by the Senufo historian Ouattara Tiona in a scholarly publication of the Institute of African History, Art, and Archaeology, University of Abidjan; see "Nomenclature de quelques termes usuels des traditions orales senufo de Côte d'Ivoire," *Les Cahiers de L'I.H.A.A.A.*, no. 2 (Abidjan, 1981), pp. 58–59. Field data that I have collected over a period going back to 1970 has enabled me to have some understanding of the complexity of the Senufo concept of "Ancient Woman," who must ultimately be seen as a mystery in the religious sense of the word. The authority of Ancient Mother, who is spirit (but not a god), is vested in the designated male leadership of the Poro Society in each sacred grove membership, and "her work" is carried out by initiates (her "children") and elders. The secret name for a certain type of sacred drum is *Maléëò* in some Poro groups, and in others the same word becomes the title of the elder selected to administer fines and penalties. Such secondary explanations of *Maléëò* or *Kaceleëò* are but partial revelations of the nature of the guiding spirit of each sacred grove, which is viewed as the "courtyard" of "Ancient Woman." Also at the center of each Poro Society is a secret "fetish" or power instrument, its components known only to a few men in each generation.

10. Portions of this essay describing the load-bearing posture, the tradition of ceremonial female drum-carriers, and the Fodombele women's Tyekpa Society drums are excerpts from Anita J. Glaze, "Senufo Woman and Art: A Caryatid Drum," a brochure pub-

lished by The Art Institute of Chicago in connection with an exhibition of the same title, organized by Ramona Austin and the author (Apr. 27–Oct. 27, 1991).

11. See Holas, *L'Art sacré senoufo* (note 7), p. 52; P. Knops s.m.a., *Les Anciens Senufo, 1923–1935* (Berg en Dal, 1980), p. 173; and T. Garrard, cat. entry in Barbier (note 2), vol. 2, p. 35.

12. P. Knops s.m.a., "Instruments de Musique de l'Afrique occidentale," *Bulletin de la Société royale belge d'anthropologie et de Préhistoire*, no. 79 (Brussels, 1968), pp. 47–48 (my translation).

13. Gilbert Bochet, "*Pliwo'o* Drum," in Barbier (note 2), vol. 2, p. 36.

14. G. Clamens, "Notes d'ethnologie senoufo," *Notes africaines* 59 (1953), p. 77. Clamens correctly identified and described in meticulous detail the major "fetish" known as *Pliwoho* or *Tyebe*, including the heavy four-legged pedestal carved with bas-relief figures around the side of the round, stool-like pedestal that supported the large ceramic container for the assemblage of magical substances. Clamens's photograph of the fetish is reproduced in Till Förster, *Die Kunst der Senufo* (Zurich, 1988), p. 93.

15. Förster (note 14), p. 45, and Garrard (note 11). Förster provided the first published description of a four-legged drum in the context of the *co'omi* dance, which is the same tradition that I first heard described briefly in 1970 by a Fodonon from the Dikodougou district who had observed the dance in the Kafiri dialect area around Sirasso.

16. Several additional combinations of "t," "o," and "o" of varying vowel length and tone could be listed, such as the verb "to fall." See Richard Mills, "Dictionnaire senoufo-francais (Cebaara)" (forthcoming, Abidjan, 1993). My translation of *tonbinge* as "association-drum" is based on statements by respondents in four different dialect areas, from the Kadile at Tingrela to the Tangara near Korhogo (Mar. 1993). I consider it highly probable that *ton* is a loan word from Mande languages to the north, where it has the same meaning.

17. Knops (note 11), p. 173 (my translation).

18. Ibid.

19. Garrard (note 11).

20. I am grateful to the Tangara chief and other elders who discussed their *tonbinge* traditions and allowed me to photograph the drum (Mar. 1993). An excellent photograph of a *tonbinge* drum with attendant youth and young girls in ritual white dress is illustrated in Förster (note 14), p. 44.

21. Interview with Kadile linguistic assistant Tyemogo Koné (Tingrela, Mar. 1993).

22. Ibid.

23. Interview with Soro Gozana (Korhogo, Mar. 1993).

24. Interviews with Leeluru Yeo (Nafara area, Feb.-Mar. 1993).

25. Chris Mattison, *Lizards of the World* (New York, 1989), pp. 176–77.

26. There are at least five species of tortoise whose range includes Senufo country in northern Côte d'Ivoire: the African softshell turtle (*Trionyx triunguis*), the West African mud turtle (*Pelusios castaneus*), Bell's hinge-back tortoise (*Kinixys belliana*), and the African helmeted turtle (*Pelomedusa subrufa*). See Carl Ernst and Roger Barbour, *Turtles of the World* (Washington D.C., 1989), pp. 12–13, 17–18, 100–101, 229–30.

27. See the drum illustrated in Förster (note 14), p. 44.

ANDREOTTI, "Brancusi's *Golden Bird*: A New Species of Modern Sculpture," pp. 134–152.

I would like to thank several people who were especially helpful in the preparation of this article. I am grateful, first of all, to Charles Stuckey for encouraging me to undertake this study and for generously sharing his own research on this piece—the questions he raised strongly influenced the course of my own research. Sidney Geist, to whom I and so many others are indebted for a lifetime of work on Brancusi, graciously consented to meet with me to discuss some of my preliminary findings. His specific contributions to my thinking on Brancusi are acknowledged throughout the article. Others who were helpful include Elizabeth Brown, with whom I discussed several issues concerning the early photographs of the *Golden Bird*; Maureen Lasko of the Ryerson Library, who valiantly pursued many interlibrary loan requests; and Susan Rossen and Michael Sittenfeld, who provided continued encouragement and valuable editorial suggestions. The staffs of the New York Public Library, The Metropolitan Museum of Art, the Library of The Museum of Modern Art, and The Newberry Library are also gratefully acknowledged. Finally, I am indebted to my husband, Bart Hirsch, for assisting me with the daunting task of combing through the Quinn correspondence at the New York Public Library, for his thoughtful reading of the manuscript, and for his support.

1. The other works—six sculptures, five drawings, and one painting—by Brancusi in the Art Institute are: *Suffering* (often called *Torment II*, 1907, bronze, 1985.542), *Wisdom* (attributed to Brancusi, c. 1908, limestone, 1955.646), *Sleeping Muse* (1910, bronze, 1931.523), *Two Penguins* (1911–14, marble, 1961.1115), *Leda* (c. 1920, marble, 1953.193), *The White Negress* (1928, marble, 1966.4), *Study for "The First Step"* (c. 1907/09, pen and ink on cardboard, 1924.930), *The First Step* (1907/09, tempera on board, 1954.1353), *Head of a Woman* (c. 1909/10, pen and ink on board, 1954.1103), *The Studio* (c. 1918, pen and ink on paper, 1981.149), *Portrait of Rue Carpenter* (by 1926, black chalk on paper, 1981.302; fig. 14), and *Head of a Woman* (n. d., charcoal and graphite on paper, 1985.473).

2. New York, Brummer Gallery, *Brancusi*, exh. cat. (1926), no. 20, as *Golden Bird*, polished bronze, 1919.

3. A word should be said here about the particularly complex situation facing the student of Brancusi's work. In 1968, Albert Elsen had already remarked on the "the mass and maze of Brancusi literature and the complexity of the problems enveloping" anyone working on this artist; see Albert Elsen, review of Sidney Geist, *Brancusi, A Study of the Sculpture*, in *Artforum* (Dec. 1968), p. 70. The "mass" of Brancusi literature has only increased since then and the "maze," while benefiting from the excellent work of many writers, starting with Geist's pioneering book of 1968, still remains considerable; see Sidney Geist, *Brancusi, A Study of the Sculpture*

(New York, 1968; rev. ed., 1983). This situation has not been helped by the fact that much archival material (including letters) in Brancusi's possession at his death has been inaccessible to scholars except in the partial and unverifiable form presented in Pontus Hulten, Natalia Dumitrescu, and Alexandre Istrati, *Brancusi* (Paris, 1986; New York, 1987). If this material is ever made available, it may well resolve many of the factual questions surrounding Brancusi's work. In addition, perhaps because of the strong and varied allegiances Brancusi has inspired, the debate surrounding his art has at times taken a regrettably polarized form, pitting proponents of one view against another, a situation recently summarized in Eric Shanes, *Brancusi* (New York, 1989), p. 8.

4. Quoted from the catalogue of the Brancusi exhibition at the Brummer Gallery (note 2), n. pag.; and Carola Giedion-Welcker, *Constantin Brancusi, 1876–1957* (New York, 1959), p. 219. Brancusi's complete statement in the catalogue goes as follows: "Simplicity is not an end in art, but one arrives at simplicity in spite of oneself, in approaching the real sense of things. Simplicity is complexity itself, and one has to be nourished on its essence in order to understand its value." For earlier versions of this statement, see Hulten, Dumitrescu, and Istrati (note 3), pp. 121 and 124.

5. The earliest *Endless Column* is dated to 1918 and was followed by several variations, culminating in 1937 in the monumental *Column* at Tîrgu-Jiu in Romania. For a detailed history of this piece, see Sidney Geist, "Brancusi: The *Endless Column*," *The Art Institute of Chicago Museum Studies* 16, 1 (1990), pp. 70–87.

6. Brancusi labeled a photograph of twin bases (fig. 7), one of which was very likely this one, as "two bases African wood, yellow" ("deux socles bois d'Afrique, jaune"). See Marielle Tabart and Isabelle Monod-Fontaine, eds., *Brancusi, Photographer* (New York, 1979), pl. 23, p. 119, no. 23. See also the discussion of the base later in this essay.

7. Some of these irregularities in the limestone section of the base may also be due to subsequent restoration efforts, including the addition of an aluminum plate to the underside of this section (see condition reports in the files of the Department of Twentieth-Century Painting and Sculpture at the Art Institute). The limestone from which this section was carved seems to have been very friable from the start. One of the upper edges is already visibly damaged in the two photographs of *Golden Bird* reproduced in the *The Little Review* 8 (Autumn 1921), pls. 17 and 24.

8. Mina Loy, "Brancusi's Golden Bird," *Dial* 73 (Nov. 1922), pp. 507–08.

9. Ezra Pound, "Brancusi," *The Little Review* (note 7), pp. 5–6.

10. Jeanne R. Foster, "New Sculptures by Constantin Brancusi: A Note on the Man and the Formal Perfection of His Carvings," *Vanity Fair* 18 (May 1922), p. 68. The essay Foster envisioned on the *Birds* was eventually written by Athena Tacha Spear; see *Brancusi's Birds* (New York, 1969).

11. Loy (note 8).

12. See the discussion of the date later in this essay.

13. That Brancusi took some pride in this work, even after he had renounced the artistic goals it represented, is demonstrated by his

inclusion of it in the major photographic coverage of his work presented in the inaugural issue of the journal *This Quarter* 1, 1 (1925), Art Supplement, n. pag., where it is reproduced as "*Ecorché. Modèle accepté à l'Ecole de Médicine et des Beaux-Arts, Roumanie, 1903*" ("*Anatomical Figure. Model accepted at the Ecole de Médicine et des Beaux-Arts, Romania, 1903*"). This issue represented the most extensive visual coverage of Brancusi's work up to that time, as it included forty photographs in addition to five reproductions of Brancusi's drawings.

14. Brancusi was apparently enrolled at the Ecole des Beaux-Arts in the studio of Mercié in 1905 (Geist [note 3], p. 2). Geist has traced the probable impact of a number of major artistic events on Brancusi's work of these years, including the Gauguin retrospective of 1906, which included distinctly primitivistic carvings in wood and stone; the exhibition in 1907 of Derain's primitivistic carving *Crouching Figure*; the viewing of important works by Matisse at the Salon d'Automne of 1907; and the increasingly primitivistic character of the work of many avant-garde artists, such as Derain, Matisse, Picasso, and Vlaminck. See Geist, *Brancusi/The Kiss* (New York, 1978), pp. 30 ff.; and his essay "Brancusi," in New York, The Museum of Modern Art, "*Primitivism*" *in 20th Century Art: Affinity of the Tribal and the Modern*, exh. cat. (1984), vol. 2, pp. 345–67.

15. While Brancusi understood his need to become independent of Rodin, he later acknowledged that "Without the discoveries of Rodin, my work would have been impossible"; quoted in Geist (note 3), p. 141. Brancusi was probably referring to Rodin's daring truncations of the human figure, often referred to as "partial figures," which encouraged him to take liberties of his own, especially toward a radical simplification of his forms.

16. Cited in Geist, *Brancusi/The Kiss* (note 14), p. 9, which should be consulted for a thorough consideration of this work and the circumstances leading up to it.

17. Ibid., pp. 22–24. Important variations on Brancusi's version were to follow in fairly quick succession in 1908, 1909, and 1912 (ibid., figs. 39–43).

18. "Direct carving is the true path toward sculpture, but also the worst one for those who don't know how to walk. And in the end, direct or indirect carving doesn't mean a thing—it's the finished work that counts!" See *This Quarter* (note 13), p. 235. Further statements by Brancusi on this topic are gathered in Spear (note 10), pp. 22–24. For more on the significance of direct carving and the mystique of truth to the material, see Geist, *Brancusi/The Kiss* (note 14), pp. 4–9; and Albert Elsen, *Origins of Modern Sculpture: Pioneers and Premises* (New York, 1974), pp. 120–30. See also Spear (note 10), p. 23 n. 13; and Geist's essay in "*Primitivism*" *in 20th Century Art* (note 14), p. 367 n. 1, for a list of works by Brancusi that are exceptions to this otherwise exclusive commitment to direct carving.

19. Spear (note 10), p. 23. I discussed this point as recently as December 1992 with Sidney Geist, who was adamant that the bronze version of *Golden Bird* would have necessarily followed a carved version. As he put it, this was as inevitable as "night follows day."

20. Sidney Geist believes that the Art Institute's *Golden Bird* was derived from *Yellow Bird*, a view embraced most recently by Friedrich Teja Bach. See New York, The Solomon R. Guggenheim Museum, *Constantin Brancusi, 1876–1957: A Retrospective Exhibition*, exh. cat. by Sidney Geist (1969), p. 94; and Friedrich Teja Bach, *Constantin Brancusi: Metamorphosen plastischer Form* (Cologne, 1987), p. 457, no. 155. Spear (note 10), p. 46, was instead of the opinion that *Golden Bird* derived from a lost marble.

21. See Spear (note 10), pp. 9–10.

22. For an extended treatment of this folk tradition and its relation to an even broader tradition of solar birds, see ibid., pp. 4–8. Brancusi himself apparently once described the story referred to in the title of his first *Bird* in the following words: "Prince Charming was in search of Ilena Cosinzene. The master bird is the bird that spoke and showed the way to Prince Charming"; quoted in Geist (note 3), p. 38, from Petre Pandrea, *Potrete si controverse* (Bucharest, 1945), vol. 1, p. 161.

23. "L'oiseau m'a fasciné et ne me lâche plus," quoted in Giedion-Welcker (note 4), p. 30 n. 5. See also a statement Brancusi made in 1936: "My birds are a series of objects in a central research that remains the same. The ideal realization of this object would be an enlargement to fill the vault of the sky." See Geist (note 3), p. 115.

24. Spear (note 10), pp. 53ff., catalogued twenty-eight versions, while Geist (note 3), pp. 200–201, listed twenty-seven. These figures do not include the numerous *Birds* in plaster preserved in Brancusi's studio (Musée National d'Art Moderne, Paris).

25. This is, of course, one of the reasons why Brancusi's works are so highly sought after when they do come on the market.

26. For a discussion of the symbolism of the bird in its broadest terms, see Spear (note 10), pp. 4–8. For an exploration of the personal significance of the series of birds for Brancusi, see Sidney Geist, "Brancusi's *Bird in Space*: A Psychological Reading," *Source: Notes in the History of Art* 3, 3 (Spring 1984), pp. 24–32.

27. Glenn Benge, in Peter Fusco and H. W. Janson, *The Romantics to Rodin* (Los Angeles and New York, 1980), p. 125. For a general introduction to the subject matter of late nineteenth- and early twentieth-century sculpture, see Elsen (note 18), pp. 3–13.

28. A thorough consideration of the role of animal subjects among avant-garde artists, especially sculptors, in the early part of this century far exceeds the scope of this article. Such a study would contribute, however, to a better understanding of certain shifts in subject matter during this period, shifts that are less obvious than the dramatic innovations in form, but perhaps in a number of ways no less significant. Animal sculpture enjoyed widespread popularity in the 1920s and 1930s on both sides of the Atlantic, a development to which Brancusi may well have contributed; see Tom Armstrong et al., *200 Years of American Sculpture* (New York, 1976), pp. 140–41. Conversely, Brancusi himself may have been influenced, as Sidney Geist (conversation with the author, Dec. 3, 1992) and Charles Stuckey (memo to the author, July 19, 1993) have both suggested, by the polished, simplified forms of the animal sculptor François Pompon, who started exhibiting around 1908. See, for example, Pompon's *Oie Marchant* (*Walking Goose*) of 1908, illustrated in New York, Acquavella Galleries, *François Pompon*, exh. cat. (1970), no. 11.

29. Wassily Kandinsky and Franz Marc, *The "Blaue Reiter" Almanac* (originally published in German in 1912), ed. and intro. by Klaus Lankheit (New York, 1974), p. 64.

30. Quoted in Herschel B. Chipp, *Theories of Modern Art* (Berkeley, Calif., 1968), p. 182.

31. "Sculptured corpses," cited in Giedion-Welcker (note 4), p. 220; "Les hommes nus dans la plastique ne sont pas si beaux que les crapeauds," cited in *This Quarter* (note 13), p. 236; "as ugly as a frog," cited in Geist (note 3), p. 153, from Claire Gilles Guilbert, "Propos de Brancusi," *Prisme des Arts* 12 (1957), pp. 5–7; "Art is the one thing. . .," cited in Dorothy Dudley, "Brancusi," *Dial* 82 (Feb. 1927), p. 127.

32. This plan, however, was never realized; see Spear (note 10), pp. 33–34.

33. Giedion-Welcker (note 4), p. 203.

34. *This Quarter* (note 13), p. 237.

35. See, for example, Epstein's *Doves* of 1914–15 (marble, Israel Museum, Jerusalem), Gaudier-Brzeska's *Birds Erect* (limestone, The Museum of Modern Art, New York) and *Stags* of 1914 (veined alabaster, The Art Institute of Chicago), and Duchamp-Villon's *Great Horse* of 1914 (bronze, The Art Institute of Chicago) and *Rooster* of 1916 (painted bronze, Hirshhorn Museum and Sculpture Garden, Washington, D.C.).
See Spear (note 10), pl. 45, for a possible Senufo antecedent for Brancusi's first bird. Another possible prototype for Brancusi's *Maiastra* may be found in Egyptian polished stone or bronze Horus figures, examples of which would have been available to Brancusi in the Musée du Louvre, Paris. See, for example, *Louvre: Guide des collections* (Paris, 1989), p. 92, no. 77; p. 108, no. 96; and p. 128, no.122.

36. Brancusi's list was published in Spear (note 10), p. 115. The number of sculptures belonging to each type is based on Geist (note 3), p. 200, and does not include plasters or posthumous casts. The other two versions of the second type, in addition to the Art Institute's *Golden Bird* and Yale's *Yellow Bird*, are a bronze in The Minneapolis Institute of Art, which was purchased from the artist in December 1921 (according to Friedrich Teja Bach [note 20], p. 457, no. 156), and a marble in the collection of the Baroness Alain de Gunzburg, Paris, which may actually be a later reprise of the earlier work, possibly dating to as late as the 1940s or early 1950s. Geist, in the 1983 revision of his book on Brancusi (note 3), p. 277, no. 221, dated the Gunzburg marble to c. 1923–52; Hulten, Dumitrescu, and Istrati (note 3), p. 316, no. 216, dated it to 1920?–1947; and Bach (note 20), p. 505, no. 282, dated it to c. 1923–47? For illustrations of the Minneapolis and Gunzburg *Birds*, see Spear (note 10), pls. 14, 16.

37. "J'ai voulu que la *Maiastra* relève la tête, sans exprimer par ce mouvement la fierté, l'orgeuil ou le défi. Ce fut le problème plus difficile et ce n'est qu'après un long effort que je parvins à rendre ce mouvement intégré à l'essor du vol," quoted in Ionel Jianou, *Constantin Brancusi* (New York, 1963), p. 46; "All my life. . .," cited in Giedion-Welcker (note 4), p. 198.

38. "It was about this time. . ." and "Before the Great War. . .," cited in Hulten, Dumitrescu, and Istrati (note 3), p. 92.

39. A letter from Brancusi to Quinn of May 25, 1922 (John Quinn Memorial Collection, Rare Books and Manuscripts Division, New York Public Library, Astor, Lenox and Tilden Foundations), makes it clear that the first *Rooster* was finished by early 1922, since in this letter Brancusi specifically referred to a photograph of it.

40. "C'est un oiseau encore, mais qui n'empechera pas chanter le premier, qui a attrapait [sic] le ver, en realité." See letter to Quinn of May 25, 1922 (note 39). Brancusi is generally viewed as one of those artists whose work was more or less untouched by the war, an opinion also held until recently, for instance, of Matisse. As Kenneth E. Silver has shown, however, very few artists remained or could afford to remain entirely unaffected by this experience; see Silver, *Esprit de Corps* (Princeton, N.J., 1989). Brancusi's own patriotism is evident in a letter dated Oct. 4, 1916, to Walter Pach (John Quinn Memorial Collection, Rare Books and Manuscripts Division, The New York Public Library, Astor, Lenox and Tilden Foundations), in which he concluded by saying, "A moi on ne m'a pas trouvé bon pour la guerre mais je suis fort content que mon Pays le fait, la guerre" ("Me, they didn't find me good enough to go to war, but I am very happy that my country is going to war"), referring no doubt to Romania's recent entry into the war on the side of the Allied forces. The possible impact of the war on Brancusi's work is a topic that deserves further attention.

41. Early reproductions of this photograph include ones in *The Little Review* (note 7), pl. 17; *This Quarter* (note 13), pl. 26; Carl Einstein, *Die Kunst des 20. Jahrhunderts* (Berlin, 1926), p. 618; New York, Brummer Gallery, *Brancusi* (note 2), no. 20; and Jeanne Robert Foster, "'It's Clever, but Is It Art?' Is Asked by the Critics of Brancusi," *New York Herald Tribune*, Feb. 21, 1926, sec. 2, p. 4. A print of this photograph belongs to The Metropolitan Museum of Art, New York; see fig. 5 in the present essay. A close inspection of this print failed to identify the objects reflected on the bird's surface with any degree of certainty. Comparison of two photographs in *The Little Review*, pls. 17 and 24, identifies this securely as a photograph of the Art Institute's *Golden Bird*, rather than of the similar bronze version now in Minneapolis (see note 36). Pl. 24 is clearly a photograph of the Art Institute's *Golden Bird*, as demonstrated by its limestone base, which is fully visible here and differs in its lower section from that of the Minneapolis bird; and pl. 17 is clearly a photograph of the same *Bird*, because its limestone base, while only visible here in its upper portion, shows, at the Bird's lower left, the same slightly damaged rim as in pl. 24.

42. Man Ray, *Self Portrait* (New York, 1963), p. 209.

43. In one of Brancusi's photographs, this effect is carried to the point of almost obliterating the sculpture; see Tabart and Monod-Fontaine (note 6), pl. 26.

44. Brancusi himself defined "high polish" as "a necessity which relatively absolute forms demand of certain materials. It is not compulsory; indeed it is very harmful to those who do *bifteck* [beef steak] sculpture." See *This Quarter* (note 13), p. 235. Brancusi's first works in polished bronze seem to have been, not surprisingly, four of the *Maiastras*, this type of finish presumably being chosen to simulate the dazzling plumage for which the bird was known. These are now in the Tate Gallery, London; the Graham Collection, Washington, D.C.; the Peggy Guggenheim Collection, Venice; and the Des Moines Art Center, respectively. Brancusi subsequently applied this type of finish to several other works before turning to *Golden Bird*: *Mlle Pogany I*, 1913 (Museum of Modern Art, New York); *The Newborn I*, 1915 (Philadelphia Museum of Art); *The Muse*, 1917 (Museum of Fine Arts, Houston), and 1918 (Portland Art Museum); and *Torso of a Young Man I*, 1917 (Cleveland Museum of Art).

45. See Hulten, Dumitrescu, and Istrati (note 3), p. 25; and Geist (note 5), pp. 74–79.

46. Cited in Spear (note 10), p. 35, from G. Schildt, "Colloqui con Brancusi," *Biennale di Venezia* 8, 32 (1958), p. 24. For a general introduction to the various approaches to the base adopted by early twentieth-century sculptors, see Elsen (note 18), pp. 114–20.

47. Taking his impulse from African art, which awakened memories of the tradition of wood carving of his native Romania, Brancusi started around 1913 to make an increasing number of sculptures and bases in wood. *The First Step* of 1913 is Brancusi's first recorded sculpture and base in wood. Before then, the bases for his sculptures, however imaginative (see fig. 5), seem to have been in stone. As Charles Stuckey has suggested, the bases mentioned in a letter to Quinn of December 17, 1917, may be among Brancusi's earliest wood bases; see Hulten, Dumitrescu, and Istrati (note 3), p. 112. Brancusi also referred to "wood pieces. . .begun before the war" in a rough draft of a letter to Quinn of December 1918; see Hulten, Dumitrescu, and Istrati (note 3), p. 122.

48. There is considerable debate among Brancusi scholars regarding the role and status of these bases. Some scholars (such as Sidney Geist) consider the bases interesting but secondary by-products of Brancusi's sculptural activity, in the same order as picture frames. Others (such as Edith Balas, "The Sculpture of Brancusi in the Light of His Rumanian Heritage," *Art Journal* 35, 2 [Winter 1975/76], p. 98) consider the bases, as well as the other artifacts Brancusi produced in some number (wooden benches, doorways, stools, etc.), to be as important as his sculptures. This aspect of Brancusi's sculptural activity has even been the subject of an exhibition conceived by the artist Scott Burton; see New York, The Museum of Modern Art, *Artist's Choice: Burton on Brancusi*, exh. brochure (1989). What contributes to the confusion of roles is that some sculptures seem to have started out as bases (*Endless Column*, for example). Some of the bases, moreover, such as the one accompanying the Art Institute's *Golden Bird*, are signed (both wood components of the base bear Brancusi's monogram). And Brancusi did exhibit and sell his bases and furniture pieces; see, for example, nos. 16, 38–42, which are listed as bases, in the 1926 catalogue of the Brancusi exhibition at the Brummer Gallery, New York (note 2), and nos. 21–23, 42–43, which are listed as stools or benches, in the catalogue of the Brancusi exhibition held in the same gallery in 1933–34. On the other hand, it is also evident that the relation of a sculpture to its base was often fluid. Sculptures such as *Golden Bird* have not infrequently been exhibited on several different bases over the course of their history.

49. A still further installation of *Golden Bird* in Brancusi's studio is shown in a photograph taken around 1920 by Edward Steichen; see Geist (note 5), p. 78, fig. 13. In this photograph, *Golden Bird* is placed on what was to become the plaster capital of *The Column of the Kiss*; see Hulten, Dumitrescu, and Istrati (note 3), p. 309, no. 183.

50. In a letter to Brancusi of Nov. 5, 1920 (John Quinn Memorial Collection, Rare Books and Manuscripts Division, New York Public Library, Astor, Lenox and Tilden Foundations), Quinn specifically insisted that bases be included in the price of purchase for the two versions (bronze and marble) of *Golden Bird* and the two versions of *Mlle Pogany II*, even though Brancusi's initial offer made no mention of these. Quinn wrote, with somewhat legalistic repetitiveness:

And now I come to another thing which I think is important, namely, that this [price] includes the stone base for the marble Pogany and the bronze of the Pogany, as well as the bases for the bronze bird [*Golden Bird*] and the colored marble bird [*Yellow Bird*]. In the photograph of the bird in colored marble there was a small stone base in three sec-

tions, and then a wooden base in two sections, and then the marble base which you had indicated by a cross, marked in red ink. I assume you will send to me the three bases.

I assume also that you will send me the base for the colored marble Pogany as shown in the photograph. I also assume that you will send me the base for the bronze bird as shown in the photograph.

Unfortunately, none of the photographs Quinn refers to in this and other letters seems to have been preserved. The Quinn Art Ledger, vol. 2 (Thomas F. Conroy Collection, San Mateo, Calif., microfilmed by the Archives of American Art, Washington, D.C.), confirms, however, that bases were purchased for these works (see the files of the Department of Twentieth-Century Painting and Sculpture at The Art Institute of Chicago for a copy of the relevant portions of the art ledger, which were kindly provided by Judith Zilczer).

51. "Quel domage qu'on n'a pas pus [*sic*] plasser [*sic*] les sculptures plus eloigné [*sic*] du mur." Letter from Brancusi to Quinn preserved in the Jeanne R. Foster-William M. Murphy Collection, Rare Books and Manuscripts Division, New York Public Library, Astor, Lenox and Tilden Foundations. A list accompanying this letter and published in Hulten, Dumitrescu, and Istrati (note 3), p. 147, identifies number 7 as "two bases, yellow wood, 3,000 Frs for both." A 1922 entry in the Quinn Art Ledger (note 50) identifies number 7 as "two bases," and the current base of *Golden Bird* is indeed inscribed "7" twice on the underside of the rectangular wood component. The entry in the Quinn Art Ledger appears in vol. 2, p. 66, preceding an entry dated August 4, 1922 (see copy in the files of the Department of Twentieth-Century Painting and Sculpture at the Art Institute). Charles Stuckey first identified photograph no. 7 and suggested its correspondence to the "7" on the base of *Golden Bird*.

Particularly instructive about Brancusi's general attitude toward the base is a group of hitherto unpublished photographs originating from the Brummer Gallery in New York where Brancusi had two major one-person shows, in 1926 and 1933–34. These photographs (which now belong to Sidney Geist, who generously shared them with me) seem to have served as tools in planning the second of the two Brummer Gallery shows, the biggest one-person exhibition of Brancusi's sculptures up to that time. Scribbled on the back of the photographs are instructions in Brancusi's hand regarding the placement of the pieces on various bases, instructions such as *non dépareiller* (do not separate) and *à volonté* (at will), indicating that in some cases Brancusi wished the sculpture to remain on the base shown in the photograph, while in others he specified a degree of flexibility. These photographs testify to Brancusi's continual experimentation in the placement of his works. They also suggest that anything but the broadest generalizations about Brancusi's attitude toward the base have limited significance, since he clearly tailored his solution to the individual requirements of each sculpture, deciding on a case-by-case basis if a base was necessary and if some flexibility was tolerable in the exhibition of a piece.

52. For the most thorough treatment of Quinn's art collecting, see Hirshhorn Museum and Sculpture Garden, Washington, D.C., *"The Noble Buyer": John Quinn, Patron of the Avant-Garde*, exh. cat. by Judith Zilczer (1978). Other valuable sources are Aline B. Saarinen, *The Proud Possessors* (New York, 1958); and B.L. Reid, *The Man from New York: John Quinn and His Friends* (New York, 1968).

53. For example, among the pieces that once belonged to Quinn and that are now in the Art Institute are two of Picasso's most well-known works, *The Old Guitarist* of 1903 and *Mother and*

Child of 1921, as well as Matisse's still life *Apples* of 1916. For more information on the Armory Show, especially on its Chicago showing, see Andrew Martinez, "A Mixed Reception for Modernism: The 1913 Armory Show at The Art Institute of Chicago," *The Art Institute of Chicago Museum Studies* 19, 1 (1993), pp. 30–57.

Although very much ahead of his time in his taste for the most daring contemporary literature and art, Quinn also showed himself to be very much a man of his time in his often tyrannical use and pursuit of power and in his prejudices, especially his fierce anti-Semitism. His voluminous and in many respects fascinating correspondence, preserved today in the New York Public Library, is peppered with crude anti-Semitic remarks and suggests that Quinn's collecting, however dazzling in its results and beneficial to individual artists, was not fueled solely by lofty ideals and generous impulses, but also by strong antagonisms and prejudices. This mixture of motives is reflected in a letter to Ezra Pound of July 27, 1915, in which Quinn wrote, "I agree with all you wrote about *not* buying the work of the dead old ones but live work by living men. . . .I prefer the bite and harshness of new work to the glossy sleek stuff the Jew dealers and traders and fakirs like Berenson exploit" (John Quinn Memorial Collection, Rare Books and Manuscripts Division, New York Public Library, Astor, Lenox and Tilden Foundations).

54. In a letter to Epstein of July 27, 1914, Quinn asked the sculptor, "What do you think of Brancusi's work? I have a head in marble of Madame [*sic*] Pogany and also a mythological bird in marble [*Maiastra* of 1910–12]." Epstein responded, "I can without reserve say that Brancusi is indeed a fine sculptor. I have the greatest admiration for his work. The good sculptors now in the world are few at the most—only three or four I think," an opinion that Quinn quoted to Pach in a letter of Aug. 25, 1914. Both of the above letters are in the John Quinn Memorial Collection, Rare Books and Manuscripts Division, New York Public Library, Astor, Lenox and Tilden Foundations. The first letter from Brancusi to Quinn in the John Quinn Memorial Collection, New York Public Library, is dated Jan. 19, 1917.

55. See letters from Brancusi to Quinn of Dec. 27, 1917; from Quinn to Brancusi of Oct. 26, 1918; and rough drafts from Brancusi to Quinn of Dec. 1918 and Jan. 24, 1919 (published in Hulten, Dumitrescu, and Istrati [note 3], pp. 111–12, 120–21). In this last letter, Brancusi emphasized that "the important thing for me would be to see my works brought together."

56. In a letter to Pach of Feb. 28, 1916, Quinn commissioned *The Kiss*. He indicated that he had obtained the right of first refusal in a letter to Pach of Sept. 8, 1916. On the same day, he wrote to Epstein about his four most recent acquisitions. He commissioned the bronze *Muse* in a letter to Brancusi of Mar. 14, 1917, and this same commission was discussed in a letter from Brancusi to Quinn of June 20, 1917. All of the above letters, including the letter to Yeats, are in the John Quinn Memorial Collection, Rare Books and Manuscripts Division, New York Public Library, Astor, Lenox and Tilden Foundations.

There are also three letters of 1916, quoted in Hulten, Dumitrescu, and Istrati (note 3), pp. 106–107, which make mention of a *Golden Bird*. Since these letters might at first be thought to refer to the Art Institute's *Golden Bird*, it seems important to consider them at least briefly here. Two of these letters are from Brancusi to the dealer Marius de Zayas, while the third is from Pach to Brancusi. In the first of these, dated Sept. 13, 1916, Brancusi wrote to de Zayas that the "*Golden Bird* is ready, and for you the price is 1000 francs." On the following Oct. 31, Brancusi again wrote to de

Zayas, "In your letter of September 28 you mentioned nothing about the *Golden Bird*, and when I got your cable, I didn't have it anymore. I explained this to your brother Georges, who came to see me. I do hope there has been no misunderstanding." Finally, in an undated letter of 1916 to Brancusi, Pach referred to Quinn as "the fortunate owner of your *Golden Bird* and *Mlle Pogany*."

The *Bird* referred to in the letters to de Zayas still remains to be identified: none of Brancusi's recorded *Birds* fits the chronology suggested in these letters—that Brancusi offered a *Bird* to de Zayas on Sept. 13, 1916, and sold it to someone else by Oct. 31, 1916. We know that Brancusi referred to bronze versions of *Maiastra* as *Golden Bird* as early as 1911 and continued to do so as late as 1914 (see Spear [note 10], p. 13 n. 10, and opp. pl. 3; and Hulten, Dumitrescu, and Istrati [note 3], p. 285, no. 65), and that his titles were rather fluid at this time. An extensive perusal of Quinn's correspondence, moreover, has revealed no evidence that the purchase of the Art Institute's *Golden Bird* was discussed prior to 1920. It thus seems conceivable that Pach was referring in his letter to the only bird known to have been in Quinn's collection at that time, the marble *Maiastra* (fig. 4) acquired with *Mlle Pogany* in 1914.

57. The measurements given by Spear (note 10) for *Yellow Bird* (h. 36¼ in., max. circ. 20½ in., min. circ. 3⅝ in.) are slightly smaller than those for *Golden Bird* (h. 37¾ in., max. circ. 21 in., min. circ. 3¾ in.). Because *Yellow Bird* is shorter than *Golden Bird*, Spear (note 10, p. 46) asserted that the latter could not have been cast from *Yellow Bird*. It seems possible, however, that *Golden Bird* could have been cast from a reworked plaster of *Yellow Bird*, therefore explaining the differences in size.

Golden Bird has been traditionally dated to 1919, which is the date given in the catalogue of the 1926 Brancusi exhibition at the Brummer Gallery in New York. See Geist (note 3) no. 117 (no. 125 in rev. ed.); Spear (note 10), no. 8; Hulten, Dumitrescu, and Istrati (note 3), no. 108; Bach (note 20), no. 155. Other early references to the Art Institute's *Golden Bird* are as follows: reproduced twice, once as part of a studio shot, untitled and undated, in *The Little Review* (note 7), nos. 17 and 24; listed in "Contemporary French Art" held at the Sculptors' Gallery, New York, Mar. 24–Apr. 10, 1922, as no. 14, *Bird*, 1921, bronze; reproduced as *L'Oiseau d'or*, 1920, in *This Quarter* (note 13), pl. 26; reproduced as *Der goldene Vogel*, bronze, 1919, in Einstein (note 41), p. 526.

58. For the letters, note, and bill cited above, see Hulten, Dumitrescu, and Istrati (note 3), pp. 121, 122, 124, and 135, respectively. I am indebted to Charles Stuckey for suggesting this reconstruction of events.

59. A telegram Quinn sent to Brancusi on Oct. 9, 1920, acknowledges receipt of the photographs. This telegram and other excerpts from the Brancusi/Quinn correspondence in the John Quinn Memorial Collection, New York Public Library, were published by Athena Tacha Spear in *The Art Bulletin* 52, 1 (Mar. 1970), p. 111, under "Letters to the Editor." Regarding the purchase of these works, see the letter from Quinn to Brancusi of Nov. 5, 1920, as well as Quinn's Art Ledger, vol. 2, both cited in note 50 above.

While it may appear surprising that Quinn was willing to purchase both versions (marble and bronze) of these two works, several considerations may help explain his decision. First of all, the purchase of all four works at one time was a good business deal, since buying in quantity often entailed a considerable discount on the price of each individual piece, and Quinn's letters certainly show that he appreciated a good bargain. Secondly, earlier versions of the *Bird* and *Mlle Pogany* were Quinn's very first purchases of

Brancusi's work. By 1920, Quinn may well have been aware that these indeed represented two of the most important themes in Brancusi's sculpture. He may also have appreciated by then the importance of the series—of closely related versions of the same piece—for the artist. Ezra Pound, a close friend of Quinn's, clearly articulated this view about the *Birds* when he wrote in a 1921 *Little Review* article on Brancusi (note 7, p. 5), "There is perhaps six months' work and twenty years' knowledge between one model of the erect bird and another, though they appear identical in photography." Before his death in 1924, Quinn was to buy one more marble bird, *Bird in Space* of 1923 (Mrs. Wolfgang Schoenborn, New York), bringing the total number of *Birds* in his collection to four.

60. See letter from Marcel Duchamp to Brancusi of Dec. 31, 1926, in Hulten, Dumitrescu, and Istrati (note 3), p. 178.

61. See The Arts Club of Chicago, *Drawings 1916/1966: An Exhibition on the Occasion of the Fiftieth Anniversary of The Arts Club of Chicago*, exh. cat. (1966), pl. 6; The Art Institute of Chicago, *The Joseph Winterbotham Collection: A Living Tradition*, intro. by Lyn DelliQuadri (1986), p. 9, fig. 4; and The Arts Club of Chicago, *The Arts Club of Chicago: Seventy-Fifth Anniversary Exhibition, 1916–1991*, exh. cat. (1992), p. 23 (ill.).

62. As Mary Hoyt Wiborg put it in the obituary she wrote for Mrs. Carpenter in the *New York Times*, Dec. 12, 1931, "Chicago owes its *Arts Club* entirely to her initiative, a pattern that all modern clubs or art groups in this country base themselves upon." For a valuable summary of the Arts Club's history and activities, see *The Arts Club of Chicago* (note 61).

63. Chicago's first experience of Brancusi's art came at the Armory Show, which was on view at the Art Institute from Mar. 24 to Apr. 16, 1913. It included four sculptures in plaster by the artist.

64. The Minutes of the Arts Club contain the following statement: "Miss Roullier also announced that the Arts Club Gift Purchase Fund had bought 'The Bird' by the sculptor, Brancusi, for $1200, and that this sculpture would be donated at a later date to the Art Institute of Chicago" (Minutes of the Executive Committee, Jan. 27, 1927, p. 2, The Arts Club Papers, The Newberry Library, Chicago). In 1990, *Golden Bird* was sold to the Art Institute in an effort to raise funds for the Arts Club's new home, since the club was threatened with eviction from its current quarters. Among the many articles covering this story, see Richard Christiansen, "Treasured Sculpture Saved for City," *Chicago Tribune*, Dec. 31, 1989, pp. 1 and 10; and Henry Hanson, "A Moveable Feast," *Chicago*, Apr. 1992, p. 81. Finally, for more on Duchamp's role as art consultant, promoter, and installation designer, see Naomi Sawelson-Gorse, "The Art Institute of Chicago and the Arensberg Collection," *The Art Institute of Chicago Museum Studies* 19, 1 (1993), pp. 80–101.

65. Letter in The Arts Club Papers, The Newberry Library, Chicago. Based on a list submitted by Duchamp to Roullier on Dec. 16, 1926, and an annotated copy of the exhibition catalogue (both in The Arts Club Papers, The Newberry Library), the Chicago show included twenty-three sculptures, one painting, and twenty-one (list) or nineteen (annotated catalogue) drawings, as opposed to thirty-six sculptures, one painting, and twenty-seven drawings included in the New York exhibition. Presumably, the works not included in Chicago were among those sold in New York. As Duchamp stated in his letter to Roullier, "L'exposition chez

Brummer c'est très bien terminée; nous avons vendu pour plus de $7000—ce que je considère un succès" ("The exhibition at Brummer's ended very well; we have sold more than $7000 worth—which I consider a success"). It is also interesting to note that there had originally been plans for the Brancusi show to go to Denver and Los Angeles. But, as Duchamp explained in his letter, "Nous n'allons pas à Denver ni à Los Angeles. Les frais les ont effrayés—et cependant j'avais essayé de ne pas être exigeant" ("We will not be going to Denver or Los Angeles. The costs scared them—and yet I tried not to be demanding").

66. Both of the above letters from Duchamp to Brancusi are published in Hulten, Dumitrescu, and Istrati (note 3), pp. 180 and 183, respectively.

67. Marguerite B. Williams, "Here and There in the Art World: Brancusi and the Moderns," *Chicago Illustrated News*, Dec. 29, 1926; C. J. Bulliet, "Sculptor's First Big Show at the Arts Club," *Chicago Evening Post*, Jan. 4, 1927; idem, "Artless Comment on the Seven Arts," *Chicago Evening Post*, Jan. 11, 1927; "Brancusi's Sculpture," *Chicago Illustrated News*, Jan. 12, 1927; Samuel Putnam, "Brancusi Doth Make E-Heggs of Us All," *Chicago Evening Post*, Jan. 18, 1927; and "Society Gulps Hard at Brancusi Eggs: Arts Club Exhibit of 'Sculpture' Evokes Weird Explanations," *Chicago Evening Post*, n.d. Copies of all of the above articles are preserved in The Arts Club of Chicago Scrapbook No. 4, The Arts Club Papers, The Newberry Library, Chicago.

68. C. J. Bulliet, "Artless Comment on the Seven Arts" (note 67).

69. See, for example, "Whatever This May Be—'It Is Not Art,'" *Chicago Herald Examiner*, Mar. 13, 1927.

70. I am grateful to Susan Rossen for bringing this show to my attention through the account of it in Nicholas Fox Weber, *Patron Saints: Five Rebels Who Opened America to a New Art, 1918–1943* (New York, 1992), pp. 45–50.

71. "A tall object. . ." quoted from A.F.C., "Harvard Society of Contemporary Art Supplements Great Display of French Art Current at Fogg Museum with Examples of More Recent Painters," *Saturday Evening Transcript*, Mar. 23, 1929; "It is safe. . ." quoted from A. J. Philpott, "French Modernist Exhibition," *Boston Globe*, Mar. 22, 1929.

72. See note 8 above.

ZELLEKE, "Harmonizing Form and Function: Mackay Hugh Baillie Scott and the Transformation of the Upright Piano," pp. 160–173.

I am especially grateful to Dr. David B. Robinson, Archivist of the Surrey Record Office, for allowing me access to the John Broadwood and Sons archive. Robert Baker and Allyson Swyny in the Record Office Reading Room were especially patient in accommodating my requests. Frances Collard, Assistant Curator of the Furniture and Woodwork Collection at the Victoria and Albert Museum, London, kindly shared collection records with me. Paul Reeves and Martin Levy each brought to my attention essential references concerning Baillie Scott. I am also indebted to Laurie Stein of the Werkbund-Archiv and to Inge Neumann.

1. The piano now at the Art Institute was published in "A Treasure Chest of Tone: A Departure in the Shape of the Upright Pianoforte," *The Artist* (Jan. 1898), p. 65; while this piano was illustrated, the text described the green-stained model exhibited for the first time by the Arts and Crafts Exhibition Society in 1896. The Art Institute's piano was also published by the Fine Arts Society, *Spring '84* (London, 1984), no. 46; and Martin Levy, "Variations on a Theme: Piano Cases Designed by M. H. Baillie Scott," *The British Antique Dealers' Association Handbook 1987* (London), pp. 14–19, fig. 4.

2. I wish to thank Kate Jerome and her colleagues at the Chicago Botanic Garden who helped identify the flora in the marquetry panels on the Art Institute's piano.

3. M. H. Baillie Scott, *Houses and Gardens* (London, 1906), p. 235.

4. Biographical details concerning Baillie Scott's life and his architectural work were drawn from James D. Kornwolf, *M. H. Baillie Scott and the Arts and Crafts Movement* (Baltimore and London, 1972).

5. Ibid., p. 5.

6. Archibald Knox, the future designer of silver and pewter for Liberty's, had himself graduated from, and then taught at, the School of Art before moving to London in 1897. Kornwolf suggested that Knox was influential in the development of Baillie Scott's watercolors. He also asserted that they collaborated on commissions for stained glass, copper fireplace hoods, and iron grates; see Kornwolf (note 4), p. 85. A. J. Tilbrook suggested that Knox worked in Baillie Scott's office part-time from 1892–96; see Tilbrook, *The Designs of Archibald Knox for Liberty & Co.* (London, 1976), pp. 11 and 29. Tilbrook suggested that Baillie Scott was instrumental in introducing Knox to Liberty, as he had been designing wallpapers and fabrics for the Regent street firm since 1893; see pp. 35 and 37.

7. John Ruskin, as cited by Baillie Scott in "On the Choice of Simple Furniture," *The Studio* 10 (Apr. 1897), p. 157; also cited in M. H. Baillie Scott and A. Edgar Beresford, *Houses and Gardens* (London, 1933), p. 59.

8. Baillie Scott, *Houses and Gardens* (note 3), p. 5.

9. M. H. Baillie Scott, "A Small Country House," *The Studio* 12 (Dec. 1897), pp. 170–71.

10. Baillie Scott, *Houses and Gardens* (note 3), p. 13.

11. M. H. Baillie Scott, "An Ideal Suburban House," *The Studio* 4 (Oct. 1894), p. 131.

12. Baillie Scott, "On the Choice of Simple Furniture" (note 7), p. 153.

13. Ibid., p. 152.

14. Hermann Muthesius, *The English House*, trans. Janet Seligman (London, 1979).

15. Ibid., pp. 47–49.

16. William Morris, in an address to the Birmingham Municipal School of Art, 1894, as quoted by Stuart Durant, *Ornament* (London, 1986), p. 215.

17. Lucy Orrinsmith, *The Drawing-Room, Its Decorations and Furniture* (1877; reprint, New York and London, 1978), pp. 107–08.

18. "Awards in 'The Studio' Prize Competitions: A Cottage Pianoforte Case," *The Studio* 1 (Mar. 1893), p. 225.

19. John F. Runciman, "The Pianoforte: Past, Present, and Future," *The Art Journal* 46 (1894), p. 146.

20. Muthesius (note 14), p. 216.

21. David Wainwright, *Broadwood by Appointment: A History* (London, 1982), p. 219.

22. Walter Crane, "Preface," Arts and Crafts Exhibition Society, *Catalogue of the First Exhibition* (London, 1888), pp. 5–10.

23. Arts and Crafts Exhibition Society, *Catalogue of the Fifth Exhibition* (London, 1896), p. 124.

24. Mabel Cox, "The Arts and Crafts Exhibition," *The Artist* 18 (1896), pp. 36–37.

25. "The Furniture of the 'Arts and Crafts,'" *The Cabinet Maker & Art Furnisher* 17 (Nov. 1896), p. 120.

26. Baillie Scott, "On the Choice of Simple Furniture," (note 7), pp. 154–55.

27. "A Treasure Chest of Tone: A Departure in the Shape of the Upright Pianoforte," *The Artist* 21 (Jan. 1898), p. 65.

28. Information on the number, decoration, and destination of all of the Manxman pianos discussed here was colated from the Index of Uprights and the Day Books on deposit at the Surrey Record Office. I am indebted to Dr. David B. Robinson for his assistance in tracing the movement of these pianos, including the one in the Art Institute's collection.

29. John Broadwood and Sons, *Album of Artistic Pianofortes* (London, 1895), p. 30.

30. *London Post Office Street Directory* (1902). I wish to thank Frances Collard for bringing this reference to my attention, and for fleshing out information regarding H. and J. Cooper.

31. I am grateful to Anne Escott, Acting Local Studies Librarian, Mitchell Library, Glasgow, for supplying information on Paterson, Sons and Company.

32. The piano was sold by the estate of Ernest Harris's daughter Mrs. Harries prior to being purchased by the Art Institute from H. Blairman and Sons.

33. The commission was published by Baillie Scott on several occasions: in *The Building News*, July 23, 1897; twice in *The Studio* 14 (July 1898), pp. 91–97, and 16 (Mar. 1899), pp. 107–15; and in *Houses and Gardens* (note 3), pp. 235–39. In his writings, Baillie Scott gave full credit to the Guild of Handicraft for executing his designs for furniture, going so far as to name the individual Guild cabinetmakers and metalworkers responsible. He also credited the design of the electric light fittings to Charles Robert Ashbee.

34. Alan Crawford, *C. R. Ashbee: Architect, Designer and Romantic Socialist* (New Haven, Conn., 1985), pp. 30–31, citing Ashbee, "Proposal" (undated).

35. M. H. Baillie Scott, "Some Furniture for the New Palace, Darmstadt," *The Studio* 14 (July 1898), p. 94.

36. M. H. Baillie Scott, "Decoration and Furniture for the New Palace, Darmstadt," *The Studio* 16 (Mar. 1899), p. 108.

37. Baillie Scott, *Houses and Gardens* (note 3), p. 235.

38. Baillie Scott, "Some Furniture for the New Palace, Darmstadt" (note 35) p. 93; the debt to Ashbee was noted by Crawford (note 34), p. 283.

39. Baillie Scott, "Some Furniture for the New Palace, Darmstadt" (note 35), p. 93. The tapestry, designed by Burne-Jones and made by Morris and Company, was one of a series woven for Stanmore Hall between 1891 and 1894. It was illustrated in *The Studio* 3 (July 1894), p. 98.

40. There is some confusion in determining the date by which this piano arrived at Darmstadt. Interior views of the completed rooms at Darmstadt, including one with the "Manxman" in situ, were published in Berlin in 1898 in a portfolio of plates entitled *Möbel und Zimmereinrichtungen der Gegenwart.* An interior view of the sitting room, published by Baillie Scott in 1899, shows a conventional upright piano; the "Manxman" piano is included only as a colored drawing: see Baillie Scott, "Decoration and Furniture for the New Palace, Darmstadt" (note 36), pp. 111 and 113.

41. Three months later, on May 14, 1902, this piano (number 95399), identified as being designed by M. H. B. Scott Esq., was packed for shipment, along with piano number 95406 designed by C. R. Ashbee, and sent to "The Director of the National Museum of Decorative Art, Budapest, Hungary" for show at the International Exhibition held from September to November 1902 in that city. They were returned on January 31, 1903, as "damaged." Later that year, on November 17, 1903, Baillie Scott's piano, described as being "black and purple," was taken on hire to London for exhibition at the Woodberry Gallery, 37 New Bond Street, for a period of less than two months. The piano was apparently unsold until October 20, 1910, when Broadwood records indicate that piano no. 95399, identified (incorrectly) as an "Ashbee" design, was sold for £42 less 10%, along with another upright, to J. C. Sherwin and Son, Market Square, Hanley, Staffs. The Victoria and Albert's piano still bears a metal label for "J. C. Sherwin & Sons, Hanley, Est. 1855."

42. *Furniture Made at The Pyghtle Works Bedford by John P. White Designed by M. H. Baillie Scott,* sales cat. (Bedford, 1901), p. 8.

43. Ibid., pp. 7–8.

44. Ibid., p. 5.

45. Ibid., no. 59.

46. "Studio-Talk," *The Studio* 32 (1904), p. 240.

47. The Pyghtle Works was responsible for the luxury furnishings made for a house in the country for the Swiss industrialist Theodor Bühler in Uzwill that Baillie Scott was commissioned to build and furnish between 1907 and 1911. For a detailed discussion of this commission, see Katharina Medici-Mall, *Das Landhaus Waldbühl von M. H. Baillie Scott* (Bern, 1979).

48. Crawford (note 34), pp. 288–89.

49. Sotheby's, London, *Decorative Arts Including Arts and Crafts, Art Nouveau, Art Deco, Art Pottery and Studio Ceramics* (May 16, 1986: lot 134).

50. Arts and Crafts Exhibition Society, [Catalogue of the Seventh Exhibition] (1903), no. 494, p. 183.

51. Lionel Lambourne, *Utopian Craftsmen: The Arts and Crafts Movement from the Cotswolds to Chicago* (London, 1980), p. 102.

52. Hugh B. Philpott, "The Piano Aesthetically Considered," *The Artist* 32 (1901), p. 188.

53. "Furniture," *The Studio Year-Book of Decorative Art* (1906), p. 67.

54. Muthesius (note 14), pp. 218.

55. William Dale, "The Artistic Treatment of the Exterior of the Pianoforte," *Journal of the Society of Arts* 55 (Feb. 15, 1907), p. 365.

56. George Rose, response to Dale (note 55), in *Journal of the Society of Arts* 55 (Feb. 15, 1907), p. 371.

57. "Art in Pianofortes," *The Artist* (Oct. 1, 1883), p. 323.

ULAK, "Japanese Works in The Art Institute of Chicago: Five Recent Acquisitions," pp. 174–185.

1. In offering a highly abbreviated description of the relationship between the Kamakura government and Zen, it is difficult "to elude the trap set by storytellers of the heroic" (Jeffery P. Mass, *Antiquity and Anachronism in Japanese History* [Stanford, Calif., 1992], p. 18). In fact, elements of the Kyoto aristocracy displayed a genuine interest in the spiritual aspects of Zen and, because the aristocracy did not want to be politically outflanked by the shogun, it offered patronage to Zen monks. This process of co-opting combined with the government's close monitoring of Zen at least seemed to prevent Zen monasteries from amassing military forces, a pattern seen in other sects. See Martin Collutt, "Zen and *Gozan*," in John W. Hall et al., eds., *The Cambridge History of Japan* (Cambridge, 1990), vol. 3, p. 612ff.

2. For extensive discussions of these types, see Jan Fontein and Money Hickman, *Zen: Painting and Calligraphy* (Boston, 1971); and Hiroshi Kanazawa, *Japanese Ink Painting: Early Zen Masters,* trans. Barbara Ford (Tokyo, 1979).

3. Two renderings of Daruma by the monk-artist Minchō (1352–1431) are in the collections of the Kyoto temples Tōfuku-ji and Rokuō-in. Like the Art Institute's work, these images present the patriarch in bust portraits with head and hands. Other features of these paintings bear a great similarity to the Art Institute's *Daruma.* See *Jūyō Bunkazai* (Tokyo, 1974), vol. 10, pp. 120–21.

4. Fontein and Hickman (note 2), pp. 1–5.

5. One of the earliest works of this style known in Japan is the thirteenth-century painting signed by the painter known as Ganki or Shugetsu. He seems to have been Chinese. The painting is inscribed by the Japanese monk Muzō Seishō (1234–1306); see entry 2 in *Bodhidharma* (Tokyo, 1988).

6. The general terms of this portrait suggest the work of a provincial professional artist rather than a monk painter. For example, Hasegawa Tōhaku (1539–1610), who later became a central figure in the artistic ferment of Momoyama-period Kyoto, executed Buddhist iconography, including portraits of Zen masters, while he still resided in western Japan. His well-known portrait of the warlord Takeda Shingen (1521–1573) reveals a similar juxtaposition of textile detail and dominating visage. See Nakajima Junshi, *Hasegawa Tōhaku*, in *Nihon Bijutsu Kaiga Senshū* (Tokyo, 1979), vol. 25.

7. For examples of numerous works employing similar compositional techniques, see Yamane Yuzo, ed., *Rimpa Kaiga Zenshū*, 5 vols. (Tokyo, 1977–80). This collection deals exclusively with the Kōetsu-Sōtatsu lineage.

8. Nakamura Tanio, "Jitsugetsu awabo zu," *Jidai Byōbu Shoka*, no. 88 (supplement) (Kyoto, 1990), p. 24.

9. A fine example is found in the screen attributed to Tosa Mitsunobu in the collection of the Virginia Museum of Fine Arts, Richmond. See *Muromachi Bijutsu to Sengoku gadan: Ota Dōkan kinen ten (Tokyo to teien bijutsukan)* (Tokyo, 1986), p.28; and *Nihon byōbu-e shūsei* (Tokyo, 1977), vol. 6, pp. 74–75 and 101.

10. For a discussion of theories related to these screens, see Adachi Satoshiko, "Jitsugetsu zu byobu to Musashino zu byōbu," in *Nihon Byōbu-e Shūsei* (Tokyo, 1977), vol. 9, pp. 136–44.

11. *Tales of Ise: Lyrical Episodes from Tenth-Century Japan*, trans. Helen Craig McCollough (Stanford, Calif., 1968).

12. *Sakoku*, meaning "national isolation," was a gradually evolved policy that actually began with edicts issued against foreigners, particularly missionaries, in the late sixteenth century. These edicts were unevenly enforced over a period of nearly forty years. In 1635, however, Japanese people were forbidden from leaving Japan and, in 1639, foreigners, with the exception of Dutch and Chinese traders, were forbidden entry.

13. Christine M. E. Guth, "'Varied Trees': An I'nen Seal Screen in the Freer Gallery of Art," *Archives of Asian Art* 39 (1986), pp. 48–61.

14. The images in the series are: 1. *Fishing by Torchlight in Kai Province (Kōshū hiburi)*; 2. *Tone River in Shimōsa Province (Sōshū Tonegawa)*; 3. *Chōshi in Shimōsa Province (Sōshū Choshi)*; 4. *Uraga, Sagami Province (Sōshū Uraga)*; 5. *Whaling off the Gotō Islands (Gotō kujira-tsugi)*; 6. *Fly-Hook Fishing (Kabari-nagashi)*; 7. *Noboto in Shimōsa Province (Shimōsa Noboto)*; 8. *Net Fishing in the Miyato River (Miyato-gawa naga ami)*; 9. *Fishing with Net on Poles (Machi-ami)*; and 10. *Fishing with Baskets in the Kinu River (Kinu-gawa hachi-fuse)*.

15. Parke Bernet Galleries, New York, Apr. 12, 1945: lot 37a. The provenance of the so-called Garland set has interesting Chicago connections. The set was known to have been owned by the Spaulding family, whose collection now forms a major portion of Japanese print collection in the Museum of Fine Arts, Boston. The Spauldings met Frank Lloyd Wright in January 1913, some eight months before the death of Chicago businessman Clarence Buckingham. Records suggest that about three hundred prints were sold by Wright to Buckingham, the majority of which were works by Hiroshige. In September of that year, the Spauldings inquired through Wright about the disposition of the Buckingham collection following Buckingham's death. In the ensuing eight years, the Spauldings arranged for Wright to be a principal supplier of prints to them. It is unclear whether or not the *Chie no umi* series was purchased through Wright. In any case, the Spauldings apparently sold the set to Frederick Gookin, the first keeper of the Buckingham Collection at the Art Institute. It is assumed that Gookin acquired these for his personal collection. Eventually, the series passed to the Garland collection. For an informative discussion of the Wright-Buckingham relationship, see Julia Meech, "Frank Lloyd Wright and The Art Institute of Chicago," *Orientations* (June 1992), pp. 64–76.

16. Christie's, New York, Sept. 22, 1983: lots 108–17.

17. The lot numbers for the prints acquired by the Art Institute were 112 (*Fishing by Torchlight in Kai Province*), 113 (*Whaling off the Gotō Islands*), and 117 (*Chōshi in Shimōsa Province*).

18. See Narazaki Muneshige, "Chie no umi (Hokusai ga) ni tsuite," *Ukiyo-e Art* 12 (Dec. 1966), pp. 34–40.

19. Roger S. Keyes, *Japanese Woodblock Prints: A Catalogue of the Mary A. Ainsworth Collection*, exh. cat. (Oberlin, Ohio, 1984), p. 42. Keyes wrote that the earliest known use of Prussian blue occurred in a privately commissioned *surimono* (see note 21 below) by Nagayama Koin (1765–1849) dated 1825. See cat. no. 439, pl. 140.

20. Matthi Forrer, *Hokusai* (London, 1991). See discussion of nos. 47 and 49.

21. Keyes (note 19), p. 90. Keyes offered a very satisfactory definition of *surimono*: "Meaning literally 'a printed object,' it was later used to describe certain kinds of private publications rather than commercially published woodblock prints. Originally the word was applied to prints published by members of poetry groups for private distribution; gradually it was used to describe prints which were used to announce or commemorate certain events, like musical performances. What these prints shared, besides their circumstances of private publication, was an important printed text."

22. The author is indebted to Sebastian Izzard of Christie's, New York, for this observation and for other information concerning the 1983 sale.

23. For a helpful listing of collectors and their remarks, see Christie's, New York, *Fine Japanese Prints, Paintings, Screens, and Works of Art* (Sept. 22–23, 1983), p. 39.

24. Hokusai's fame in the West was secure before his death and, remarkably, even before the Meiji Restoration (1868) and Japan's reopening to the outside world. His fame was owed in part to the accolades of Philipp Franz von Siebold (1796–1866), a Bavarian physician, naturalist, and ethnographer employed by the Dutch at their trading station in Nagasaki. In a carefully supervised visit to Edo in 1826, Siebold may have met Hokusai, or at least had indirect communication with him. A series of paintings attributed to Hokusai that is now in the Rijksmuseum voor Volkenkunde, Leiden,

was commissioned by Siebold. These paintings were executed on Dutch paper, and display an understanding of Western techniques of perspective, modeling, and chiaroscuro. Hokusai's fascination with Western representational techniques, however, certainly preceded his possible encounter with Siebold. It is instructive to view these paintings in terms of the dramatic compositions and odd palettes found in some of the prints in the *Chie no umi* series. See Willem van Gulik, "Fifteen Paintings by Hokusai in the Von Siebold Collection," in *Philipp Franz von Siebold's Ukiyo-e Collection: An Introduction* (New York, 1978), pp. 35–47; and *Philipp Franz von Siebold's Ukiyo-e Collection* (Tokyo, 1978), vol. 3, pp. 8–37.

TRAVIS, "Paul Strand's *Fall in Movement*," pp. 186–195.

This essay is written in honor of James N. Wood, who appreciated Strand's garden photographs while director of the St. Louis Museum of Art, and who on coming to The Art Institute of Chicago as director in 1980 made it possible to purchase many magnificent Strand photographs for the permanent collection.

Since 1980, the Art Institute has acquired thirty-six photographs by Paul Strand. Twelve purchases were made through the Ada Turnbull Hertle Fund. Gifts were received from Helen Harvey Mills, Walter Rosenblum, and the Paul Strand Foundation.

The print of *Fall in Movement* was made by Richard Benson after Strand's death. Before Strand died, Benson had made a master set of the prints in *Portfolio Three* and *Portfolio Four* that Strand approved. These then became the guide prints for the completion of the portfolios.

My appreciation of Strand's work and career has been helped by Walter and Naomi Rosenblum, Michael E. Hoffman, Sarah Greenough, and Kaspar M. Fleischmann. I am also grateful for the assistance of Sylvia Wolf, Colin Westerbeck, Anthony Montoya, Catherine Duncan, and Lori Singer in the preparation of the manuscript.

1. A group of Strand garden photographs were shown after his death at the Philadelphia Museum of Art in an exhibition organized by Michael E. Hoffman entitled "Paul Strand, Discoveries: The Early Years 1915–1916; and Garden Images, 1956–1974"; the exhibition ran from November 12, 1978, to June 30, 1979. In November 1992, an exhibition selected exclusively of Strand's Orgeval garden photographs was presented at the Virginia Zabriskie Gallery, Paris. This exhibition was accompanied by an illustrated booklet with an introduction by Catherine Duncan.

2. In 1926, Strand took a vacation to Colorado, where he took at least one natural still life that he included in comprehensive retrospectives of his work.

3. Paul Strand, introduction to *Portfolio One*, "On My Doorstep," 1976; also quoted in Zurich, Galerie Zur Stockeregg, *Paul Strand*, exh. cat. ed. by Kaspar Fleischmann (1990), vol. 2, p. 42.

4. Quoted in Calvin Tomkins, "Profiles: Look to the Things around You," *The New Yorker* (Sept. 16, 1974), p. 34; reprinted in *Paul Strand: Sixty Years of Photographs* (Millerton, N.Y., 1976), pp. 15–35.

5. Strand is described as "remote and austere" in Naomi Rosenblum, *Orgeval: A Remembrance of Paul Strand* (New York, 1990), p. 7. The "doggedness and suspension with which [Strand] protects himself against conditions" is a character description from a letter from Gaston Lachaise to Alfred Stieglitz, quoted in Naomi Rosenblum, "Paul Strand: The Early Years, 1910–1932" (Ph.D. diss., City University of New York, 1978), p. 154.

6. Strand's early street portraits were taken with a lens on which was mounted a right-angle mirror or prism allowing him to photograph ninety degrees from where the camera was pointed. He had tried mounting a fake lens on the body of a Graflex camera, but it was discovered by his subjects.

7. Basil Davidson described the Orgeval garden as "admirably wild" in "Working with Strand," in Maren Stange, ed., *Paul Strand: Essays on his Life and Work* (Millerton, N.Y., 1990), p. 217.

8. Catherine Duncan has provided a full description of the Orgeval garden in "The Years in Orgeval," in Stange (note 7), pp. 231–38, and in "Paul Strand: The Garden: Vines and Leaves," *Aperture 78* (1977), pp. 46–48.

9. Strand's book on France was entitled *La France de profil* with a text in French by Claude Roy. It was published in Lausanne by La Guilde du Livre in 1952. Strand's book on the village of Luzzara, Italy, was entitled *Un paese* with a text in Italian by Cesare Zavattini. It was published by in Turin by Giulo Einaudi in 1955.

10. The title *The Apple That Fell, The Garden of Eden* (1973) is written on the verso of an original print in Paul Strand's hand. The other title is written in Hazel Strand's hand. As no other prints with metaphorical titles are in Strand's own hand, one may question whether these titles were his own. It is unlikely that after sixty years of resisting them others would take it upon themselves to assign them without his permission. Catherine Duncan, who worked with the Strands on the garden photographs, remembers that, because Paul was not able to write, the titles he created for his last works had to be recorded by Hazel.

11. Another print of *The Great Vine in Death* (1973) bears the title *The Great Vine Alive in Death* and is dated 1972.

12. See Catherine Duncan, "The Years in Orgeval," in Stange (note 7), pp. 236–38.

13. Michael E. Hoffman remembers this to be the working title of Strand's book of garden photographs.

14. Catherine Duncan proposes this idea of an open future in "The Years in Orgeval," in Stange (note 7), p. 238.

15. Only one of Strand's photographs, *Mesa Verde* (1926), exists in a mounted and signed "upside-down version"; see Steve Yates, "The Transition Years: New Mexico," in Stange (note 7), pp. 90–92.

16. Richard Benson discussed Strand's printing technique in "Print Making," in Stange (note 7), pp. 103–08; see also Kaspar Fleischmann, "Interview with Richard Benson, Photographer," in Fleischmann (note 3), vol. 2, pp. 136–54.

17. Marius de Zayas, "Photography and Artistic Photography," *Camera Work* 42/43 (Apr.-July 1913), p. 14.

MUSEUM STUDIES, Vol. 18, No. 1
*Five Centuries of Japanese Kimono:
On This Sleeve of Fondest Dreams*

This issue was prepared in conjunction with a celebrated exhibition of the Art Institute's traditional Japanese costumes. The essays in this issue delve into the cultural and art-historical background of these lavish costumes, most of which were intended for use in Noh theater. This issue also includes an introductory discussion of Noh theater, an essay on a series of prints by the Japanese master Utamaro depicting the process of silk-making, and a portfolio highlighting the Art Institute's collection of kimono pattern books. A spectacular color-plate section reproduces the costumes displayed in the Art Institute's exhibition.
Spring 1992; 104 pages; 91 illustrations (27 in color); $14.95

MUSEUM STUDIES, Vol. 18, No. 2
*British Art: Recent Acquisitions and
Discoveries at the Art Institute*

This issue focuses on the growing collection of British art at the Art Institute. A foreword by Art Institute curator Martha Tedeschi discusses the place of British art in the museum's permanent collection. The essays that follow examine a previously unknown portrait study by James McNeill Whistler, a dramatic biblical painting by Philippe Jacques de Loutherbourg, a marvelous self-portrait by Joseph Wright of Derby, a masterpiece in silver by Omar Ramsden and Alwyn Carr, and two works by members of the Pre-Raphaelite circle—Dante Gabriel Rossetti and Simeon Solomon.
Fall 1992; 88 pages; 66 illustrations; $10.50

MUSEUM STUDIES, Vol. 19, No. 1
*One Hundred Years at the Art
Institute: A Centennial Celebration*

This issue, devoted entirely to the history of the Art Institute, commemorates the 100th anniversary of the museum's renowned Michigan Avenue building. Essays discuss the revolutionary 1913 Armory Show and its tumultuous effect on Chicago; the trailblazing career of Daniel Catton Rich, distinguished director of the Art Institute from 1938 to 1958; and the ground-breaking exhibition of the Arensberg Collection of modern art at the museum in 1949. This issue also features a lavish duotone section of archival photographs documenting the history of the Art Institute from 1893 to 1933.
Spring 1993; 112 pages; 105 illustrations (40 in duotone); $14.95

MUSEUM STUDIES, Vol. 20, No. 1
*Ancient Art at The Art Institute
of Chicago*

This issue of *Museum Studies* serves as a guide to the Art Institute's new galleries of ancient art, which will open in Spring 1994. An introduction on the history of the Art Institute's ancient art collection is followed by sections covering Egyptian, Greek, Roman, Etruscan, and glass works. Additional entries on an array of ancient coins will be included in the issue. All of these superb works are accompanied by entries discussing their aesthetic quality and historical background. Approximately half of the 80 featured works are reproduced in color.
Spring 1994; 96 pages; 110 illustrations (50 in color); $14.95

MUSEUM STUDIES, Vol. 20, No. 2
*A Living Tradition: The Joseph
Winterbotham Collection at The Art
Institute of Chicago*

Joseph Winterbotham left a remarkable legacy to the Art Institute. His gift of $50,000 to the museum in 1921 stipulated that the Art Institute should assemble a collection of 35 European paintings. The unique terms of this gift have resulted in one of the most distinguished collections of 19th- and 20th-century paintings in the world. In this special issue of *Museum Studies*, an introductory essay on the Winterbotham family is followed by entries on the works in the collection. All of the featured works are reproduced in color.
Fall 1994; 96 pages; 95 illustrations (35 in color); $14.95

All issues of Museum Studies *are available from The Art Institute of Chicago Museum Shop, as well as from three additional Museum Shop locations: 900 North Michigan Avenue, fifth floor; Oakbrook Center; and Woodfield Mall. Art Institute members receive a 10% discount on all purchases at each location. For more information concerning the Museum Shops, call (312) 443-3536. Museum Studies is also available by mail from the Publications Department, The Art Institute of Chicago, 111 South Michigan Avenue, Chicago, Illinois 60603-6110 (please make checks payable to* Museum Studies). *Subscription information can be found on the inside front cover of this issue.*